Contents

Introduction

Libraries are filled with copyrighted materials. All of the printed, audiovisual, and computer program materials that are so familiar to librarians and library patrons are copyrighted, except in cases where the copyright has run out, a particular item has public performance rights, or some other special set of circumstances prevails.

If you work in a library, you probably work with copyrighted materials. If you work with copyrighted materials, you need to be knowledgeable about the laws governing them. *Libraries and Copyright Law* will help you:

- understand the copyright law
- stay within the law
- honor the rights of copyright holders
- take advantages of the special rights libraries have fought for and gained for using copyrighted materials.

What is a Copyright?

A copyright is the group of fundamental rights given to authors of creative works for a limited period of time. These are the exclusive rights of:

- reproduction
- adaptation
- publication
- performance
- display.

1

This "bundle" of rights is cumulative, and some may overlap. Together these rights constitute a "copyright."[1]

It is generally illegal for anyone other than the copyright owner or someone to whom these rights have been transferred to engage in these activities. There are a number of exceptions, or what might be considered limitations, on a copyright.

These rights are similar to the rights given to other types of property owners. In fact, copyrights are said to belong to an area of law known as intellectual property. Patents and trademarks are two other forms of protection of intellectual property.

Where Do These Rights Come From?

The power to grant this "bundle of rights" to authors and inventors comes from the United States Constitution. Although the Constitution contains neither the word "patent" nor the word "copyright," the protections provided for intellectual properties by the patent and copyright laws have their roots in Article I, Section 8, Clause 8, of that enduring document. The Constitution says that Congress has the power:

> To promote the Progress of Science and the useful Arts, by securing for limited Times to Authors and Inventors the exclusive Right to their respective Writings and Discoveries.

Because libraries are most concerned with copyright, this book is devoted to that subject, but a brief explanation of what patent and trademark laws protect will help to clarify why the three categories are needed.

What is a Patent?

Patents protect inventors' discoveries and grant strong rights to patent owners. Obtaining a patent is a rigorous process, one in which existing patents are checked for substantial similarities to the applicant's idea. Only new methods, processes, ideas, or designs are granted patents. The process is also expensive, since it requires the services of a patent attorney to be sure that nothing is overlooked. Patents are protected entirely under federal law.

There are three types of patents—utility, plant, and design patents. Protection is for a period of 14 years for design patents and 17 years for the other types.

Patents protect ideas and processes, while copyrights protect neither of these. Copyrights protect the manifestation of an idea fixed in a tangible medium, but they do not protect the idea itself.

What are Trademarks?

Trademarks can be described as logos or words that symbolize a business. The golden arches of McDonald's restaurants and the Pillsbury Dough Boy are examples of trademarks. In 1946, Congress passed the Lanham Act (formally the Federal Trademark Act) under its constitutionally granted power to regulate interstate and foreign commerce. The Lanham Act identifies different categories—trademarks, service marks, certification marks, and collective marks, as well as trade and commercial names. The term "trademark" is used as an umbrella word for all of these categories. Trademark registration is for 20 years, renewable for additional 20-year periods as long as the symbol remains in use. Protection can be lost, however, if the trademark becomes generic. If, for example, people suddenly began calling photographs in general "polaroids," the term could be declared by the courts to be a generic term, and the Polaroid Company could lose its right to that trade name.

Trademarks may be protected to some extent under state as well as federal law, something they have in common with copyrights.

Why have Copyrights?

In an early U.S. Supreme Court case, the Court found that:

> The economic philosophy behind the clause empowering Congress to grant copyrights is the conviction that encouragement of individual effort by personal gain is the best way to advance public welfare through the talents of authors ... in science and useful arts! Sacrificial days devoted to such creative activities deserve rewards commensurate with the services rendered.[2]

In other words, we need the works produced by creative people, and the best way to encourage creative activity is to make sure there is an economic benefit for those who engage in it. But what about the people who want to use the creators' products? Libraries provide a wonderful example of how the rights of authors and consumers can be balanced, if the balance is achieved carefully—and legally.

What Materials Are Covered by Copyrights?

The first copyright law passed in 1790 extended only to books, maps, and charts. Today, the list of materials covered by copyright law is much longer because the evolution of the federal copyright law through the fifth and latest version has broadened its base of coverage. Today's law encompasses literary works, musical works with any accompanying words, dramatic works with any accompanying music, pantomimes and choreographic works, pictorial, graphic and sculptural works, motion pictures, and other audiovisuals and sound recordings.

Why are Copyrights a Problem?

Copyright protection is a delicate balancing act between the rights of the creator of a work and those who wish to have access to it. Striving to keep that balance has been the goal of those who have authored the increasingly complex and comprehensive versions of copyright law over its 200-year history.

Looking at the most straightforward of situations that the copyright law covers, one could be misled into wondering how there can be any problem at all. Let's look at such an example. An author writes a book and, by contract, cedes publication rights to a publisher. The publisher produces 1,000 copies, which are sold to 1,000 different people. Half of the purchasers lend their books to friends and relatives to read. Another dozen of them give the books as gifts. The rest put their copies on bookshelves in their homes and leave them there. As a matter of fact, there are no problems in this situation. Under the copyright law, a persons owns the particular volume he or she has purchased and can lend it, give it away, even throw it away. But life is seldom this simple.

For a more common scenario, let's look at that same 1,000-copy run of a book bought by 1,000 different people, several of whom have friends who are students interested in parts of the book for a research paper. These students take the book to a copy machine and make copies of the chapter or chapters that are important to them. Then one person decides to copy a chapter and put it together with a few other writings on the same topic to make an anthology. Are these people violating the copyright law in making copies as described? Well, that depends on a number of factors. It is the purpose of this book to explain which of the activities described above, as well as some others, are within the bounds of the copyright law—and which are not.

People tend to forget that when they buy a copyrighted item, such as a book, they own the particular copy that they purchase. This is called the first sale doctrine. And while they may do many things with the purchased item, including lending it, renting it, and giving it away, making copies of the item is *not* a privilege that comes with the purchase. The right to make copies of a copyrighted item stays with the copyright owner. That simple fact is one that, if not recognized, can lead to copyright violations.

With the advent of copying machines—including those that copy audio and video tapes—the fact that copies would be made became self-evident. It also became apparent that not all copying should be prohibited. Even though there was no such provision in the early versions of the copyright law, the courts developed a doctrine of fair use to allow for copying in certain circumstances. The courts were particularly sympathetic to the needs of classroom teachers and students doing library research. Now the newest version of the copyright law actually includes some wonderful provisions allowing fair use under Section 107—a codification of the 'courts' earlier rulings. In addition, Section 108 gives very special privileges to libraries and archives.

Because the publishing industry monitors the activities of those with the special privileges granted under Sections 107 and 108, it is important that these privileges not be abused. Abusing them could lead to losing them.

Why this Book?

The authors of this book have given many workshops on the copyright law to teachers, school administrators, higher education officials, and librarians. In presenting these workshops, we have come to realize that there is a fairly widespread lack of knowledge about the provisions of the law, as well as an attitude, particularly among educators, that no one would sue a school or a library. We have enlightened many a school principal by pointing out that it is not necessary for an infringement suit to get to court for the infringer to be liable for money damages. Usually, a settlement is made quietly between author or publisher and the infringer, with small amounts of money—$1,000 or $2,000 or $3,000—being paid. Such small amounts are not worth going to court over for either side, and it is much easier to pay up than to fight. Even though individual cases may involve only small amounts of money, however, it's easy to see how two or three infringements by one institution in a given year could lead to real budget distress. In this book we stress what we call *defensive law*. Our intention is to equip readers with enough knowledge about the copyright law's restrictions and privileges to enable them to take full advantage of their legal rights.

Who Needs This Book?

This book is directed to librarians, library staff, and library governing authorities. The principles covered apply to all types of libraries—public, school, academic, and special.

Beyond the Law

Not all of the copyright questions that come up in a library setting are purely legal ones. At our workshops, for example, it is not unusual for a school librarian to ask a question such as, "What should I say to my principal when he comes into the library with a music audiotape that he wants me to copy for him?" Our answer to a question like that is always 1) it's illegal to do it so you should refuse the request but 2) be sure to phrase any refusal in a way that your job is not affected. Clearly, this is as much a political issue as it is a copyright one.

Since librarians are always being asked to violate the copyright law, in some instances knowingly, it's important to know how to educate those who feel that it's okay to break the law, as long as you don't get caught. One very effective way to discourage this attitude is to use anecdotes about real instances in which there have been copyright violations and the infringer has had to pay money damages. Several examples are included in this book. Whether citing examples or explaining legal rules, however, give your listener the benefit of the doubt. Always assume that a person making an inappropriate request is not aware of the law and simply needs educating.

Two Things to Remember

Two simple facts about copyright underlie most of the information and advice that are given in this book. First, you may do with copyrighted material anything for which you can obtain permission, always in writing, from the owner of the copyright. Getting such permission takes planning and time, but authors (and other copyright holders) are generally quite accommodating if you make a reasonable request for use of their material.

Second, there is always the possibility of paying someone to use copyrighted material. The Copyright Clearance Center was established to collect money for authors and publishers whose materials are copied on a regular basis by businesses and academic institutions. Videotapes with public viewing rights and higher-than-normal price tags are manufactured to compensate their producers for the freedom of use that the purchasers of these items enjoy.

Especially in libraries, however, these two facts cannot be applied to every situation. Library patrons often lack the time to get the required permission, and libraries generally lack the funding to pay royalties for the use of copyrighted materials. This book also covers in detail those situations in which copyrighted material may be used under the aegis of fair use as well as under those special privileges granted to libraries and archives.

Organization

This book is divided into two parts. Part I deals with the history and legal background of the copyright. Learning how the copyright law evolved is essential to understanding it. Part I also features a discussion of international copyright law and an outline of the current U.S. copyright law and how it affects libraries.

Part II deals with copyright law and specific library applications. These chapters are arranged so that they can be read individually.

Each chapter begins with a series of questions, the answers to which can be found in that chapter.

Endnotes

1. The author of a work may retain the copyright but assign one or more of the rights within copyright to another person or to a publisher. For example, an author may choose to retain the right to produce an adaptation of a work while assigning all rights to publication. An author may also include language in a contract reclaiming the publication rights after a fixed period of time—for example, a year after the work goes out of print.
2. *Mazer* v. *Stein*, 347 U. S. 201 at 219 (1954).

PART I

Copyright Law Past and Present

1
Dispelling the Myths

- *What are some of the dangerous myths people believe about copyright?*

- *Can a public library be sued for copyright infringement?*

- *If a work does not have a copyright notice can I assume that it is not copyrighted and photocopy it freely?*

- *Does the copyright law prevent libraries from forming cooperative arrangements?*

- *In addition to their economic rights, should libraries be concerned about the moral rights of authors under the copyright law?*

There are many myths that people (including librarians) seem to hold about copyright. These myths are not only erroneous, they can be very dangerous. Accepting these myths as true might cause librarians to:

- violate the copyright law and subject themselves and their libraries to substantial fines and penalties
- waive their rights
- abuse those special rights libraries have fought so hard to gain.

As important as it is to know the facts about copyright law, it is just as important—perhaps even more so—to know what is *not* true. For this reason, we have devoted the first chapter of *Libraries and*

Copyright Law to dispelling 18 of the most commonly held beliefs about U.S. copyright law and its implications for libraries. Following each "myth" is an explanation of why it is false. Later chapters explore these issues in greater detail.

Myth 1: It is not important for me as a librarian to know about the copyright law.

Of all the laws that affect libraries, the copyright law is the most pervasive in its impact. Virtually all areas of the library—from acquisitions to reference—are affected by its dictates. Librarians must be aware of the law's restrictions on their activities and must know specifically what they must do to be in compliance with the copyright law.

In addition, libraries can receive copyrights as gifts or as the result of their own creative activities. Libraries and librarians sometimes create, as well as use, copyrighted materials.

Myth 2: Copyright law only relates to photocopying.

Copyright is actually a bundle of five exclusive rights granted to its owner: reproduction, adaptation, publication, performance, and display. See Appendix A for definitions and explanations of what constitutes infringement.

In addition to reproduction (photocopying) libraries should also be concerned about:

- adaptation (for example, simplifying a computer manual for use by members of the staff)
- publication (placing excerpts of a manuscript in the library's newsletter)
- performance (showing videotapes in community rooms)
- display (showing excerpts from copyrighted works to another location using an opaque projector).

Myth 3: It is always difficult to comply with the copyright law.

This is not necessarily true. In some cases, it may only require posting a copyright warning notice:

- on or near a photocopier
- at the place where interlibrary loans are generally made
- on the package of a computer program that is circulated
- on the interlibrary loan form.

See Appendix B for the exact text and basic requirements of all notices relating to libraries required under the copyright law.

Myth 4: There is nothing that my library can do without restriction under the copyright law.

What your library *can absolutely do*[1] (as many times as you wish) with a book or other printed material, when you have a legally owned copy (one purchased from a bookseller, book jobber, or authorized reprint agent), is:

- lend it
- sell it
- give it away
- rent it
- put it on reserve
- write notes in the margin or highlight sections.

Note: These privileges are not available for other media. For example, phonorecords and computer software can no longer be rented for commercial gain. Nonprofit libraries can lend software for nonprofit purposes, provided they affix a specific warning.[2]

Myth 5: Once my library owns a copy of a book, we can do anything we want with it.

First of all, it is important to know that the phrase that applies here is, "it depends." Your library *cannot* just take that legally owned book or periodical or any part of it and:

- make a photocopy of it
- fax it
- put it on microfilm or microfiche
- convert it into a machine-readable form
- make it into an audiotape or videotape
- adapt it for use by your patrons or staff
- improve upon it or make it better and then distribute copies of that new improved edition to your patrons or staff
- paraphrase or parody it and give copies of this to your patrons or staff
- make an agreement with another library or group of libraries that they do not have to purchase the book or subscription because you will supply them with photocopies upon demand.

However, your library can do these things if it:

- fulfills certain basic requirements
- does them for certain purposes
- gets written permission from the copyright holder

- pays for the right.

One of our purposes in this book is to tell you how to fulfill these requirements, what these "certain purposes" are and under what conditions they are valid, how to get permission, and whom you can pay for these rights.

Myth 6: The copyright law prevents libraries from forming cooperative arrangements.

The copyright law does not absolutely stop a library from any legitimate activity. In addition to the rights given under the law, there is always the possibility of:

- using material in the public domain that is no longer protected by the copyright law
- requesting permission of the copyright owner
- purchasing additional copies of a work
- acquiring a copy from an authorized agent who fulfills copyright requirements
- paying a fee to the owner of the copyright or to the Copyright Clearance Center.

In terms of cooperative arrangements, the copyright law states that libraries or archives are not prevented from participating in interlibrary arrangements so long as an arrangement does not have as its purpose or effect substituting for a subscription or replacing the purchase of a work.[3] In the event that the arrangement does, libraries can arrange for purchase of additional copies or for payment of copyright fees.

Payments can be made in a number of ways—either per transaction or for an annual fee after determining average usage. There is also the option of working through professional library organizations to get the copyright law changed.

Myth 7: There are no limitations on what and how a library puts something on display.

The lawful owners of a work should be able to put their particular copy on public display without the consent of the copyright owner. This would include putting it in a display case. There are some important restrictions however, on the ability to display it indirectly, as through an opaque projector.[4] If the lawfully-owned copy itself is intended for projection, such as a photographic slide or transparency, the public projection of a *single* image would be permitted as long as the viewers are present at the place where the copy is located.[5]

The simultaneous projection of multiple images of a work (several screens), or transmission of an image to the public over television or other communication channels would be an infringement for the same reason that reproduction via copies would be.[6] It would reduce the demand for copies of the work and deprive the author of revenue. In addition, acquiring a work by loan, lease, or rental from the copyright owner does not entitle one to display it publicly, unless such permission is specifically negotiated.[7] These restrictions are intended to prevent the display from affecting the copyright owner's market for reproduction and distribution.

Myth 8: If it does not have a copyright notice on it, it is not copyrighted and can be freely copied.

To some degree, this might have been true at one time. Up until 1978, a work was not copyrighted unless it:

- bore a copyright notice like "© 19__ by _____" on the verso of the title page
- was printed in the United States
- was registered and deposited with the U.S. Copyright Office.

Today it is definitely not always easy to tell if a work is copyrighted. For example, works published after March 1, 1989 do not have to have the copyright notice to be protected. The United States also has copyright agreements with many foreign countries. Works published in any of these countries are eligible for U.S. copyright protection.

Myth 9: There are no special considerations that we have to observe concerning manuscripts in our library's own collection.

Unpublished works, particularly those that are part of the library's own collection, have some special problems. Can the work be microfilmed? Can a backup, preservation photocopy be made and the original stored away in a safe place? Can the library quote the manuscript in its publications or news releases? Like other answers to copyright questions, it depends. See Chapter 4 for more information.

Myth 10: When it comes to copyright violations, I do not have to worry about what I do not see.

One of the special rights that librarians have under the current copyright law is the privilege of not becoming "copyright police" in their libraries. This is not the same as simply ignoring what is going on or not responding to a patron's request about what might or might not be a violation. Libraries can have unsupervised photocopiers, but a copyright notice must appear near or on the machine.

Myth 11: Public libraries and their employees are not eligible to become copyright owners.

In general, works by the U.S. Government or its employees created as part of their official duties are not eligible for copyright protection, whether published or unpublished.[8] On the other hand, works created by employees of municipal or state governments in their jobs can be copyrighted.

Even for U.S. Government publications, there are some important exceptions. Does this prohibition apply to works prepared under a U.S. contract or grant?[9] What if a work was prepared by a U.S. government in a foreign country where government publications can be copyrighted?[10] What about privately prepared works published by the U.S. government[11], publications of the National Technical Information Service (NTIS)[12] and U.S. Postal Service?[13] The answers to these questions illustrate how difficult it is to make absolute statements about the copyright law. See the chapter endnotes for some answers to these questions.

Myth 12: It is possible to copyright just about anything.

There are specific things that cannot be copyrighted. Ideas, procedures, processes, systems, methods of operation, concepts, principles, or discoveries cannot be copyrighted regardless of the form in which they are described, explained, illustrated, or embodied in a work.[14] Copyright does not preclude others from using the ideas or information revealed by an author's work, but does protect the particular expression.

Blank forms, such as time cards, graph paper, account books, diaries, bank checks, scorecards, address books, report forms, order forms, and the like, that are designed for recording information and do not in themselves convey information cannot be copyrighted.[15] In addition, copyright of useful items is very limited. The industrial design of a lamp, for example, cannot be copyrighted, but that portion of the same lamp that is applied art can.[16] There are numerous restrictions governing the copyright of architectural works.[17] Currently, typefaces receive no copyright protection of any kind.[18] Nevertheless, protection for typefaces is now under consideration.

Myth 13: Public libraries cannot be sued for copyright infringement.

When the copyright law was completely revised in 1976, copyright laws became governed primarily by federal law, and jurisdiction over copyright disputes fell exclusively to federal courts. Under this system, states and municipalities could be sued for copyright infringement just like any other defendant. In 1985, the U.S. Supreme court decided a case which held that when Congress intends to abrogate state immunity from suit in federal court (sovereign immunity), it must be explicitly and unambiguously stated in the language of the statute itself.[19]

To avoid any problems, Congress passed the "Copyright Remedy Clarification Act" in 1990.[20] This Act clarifies that the intent of Congress when it passed the 1976 Copyright Act was that all defendants in copyright infringement suits, including states and municipalities, be liable for money damages.

In short, public libraries can be sued in federal court for violations of copyright laws, and statutory damages and attorneys' fees can be awarded to the plaintiffs. The full panoply of remedies are available to a copyright owner against any defendant, including state and local governments.

Myth 14: If you paraphrase a work, you are not violating its copyright.

It depends.[21] Among the rights given an author of a work under the copyright law is the right to reproduction. "Reproduction" includes the right to produce an imitation. If a paraphrase were to take an author's particular "expression" rather than just the author's idea, it would be considered an infringement.

The courts have developed several tests to help them determine if a work is being infringed upon.[22] These can be helpful in understanding what part of a work is an idea and what part is the author's protected expression.

Also, infringement may depend upon whether or not the making of the paraphrase was within fair use and would thus be permissible. For example, was the paraphrasing for a purpose such as criticism, comment, news reporting, teaching, scholarship or research? Is the paraphrasing being done for gain or for nonprofit educational purposes?[23] Is the work that is being paraphrased in a field that generally requires reference to other works, such as science? How much and of what importance to the overall work was the part paraphrased? What effect will the paraphrasing have on the potential market for the original work? Could it substitute for the original?

Myth 15: Putting a work in a compilation keeps it out of the public domain.

Copyright in a "new version" covers only the material added by the later author and has no effect one way or the other on the copyright or public domain status of the preexisting material.[24]

Myth 16: To be copyrighted, a work must be novel and ingenious and have literary merit.

There are two fundamental requirements for obtaining a copyright—originality and fixation in a tangible form. Originality here does not refer to novelty or ingenuity.

Copyright protection does not require any level of literary merit. Catalogs, directories, and similar factual, reference, or institutional works and compilations of data can be copyrighted. Originality means original to the author (that is, one work cannot be copied from another).

Myth 17: The authors of a creative work have no moral rights to their creations.

The moral rights of authors generated the most debate in Congress in 1988 when the United States debated membership in an international copyright agreement known as the Berne Convention. Moral rights here refer to non-economic rights under Article 6bis of the Convention, which provided that authors shall have the rights of paternity and integrity. Paternity is the right to be named as author of a work. Integrity is the right of authors to object to distortion or other alterations of their works, or derogatory action deemed prejudicial to their honor or reputation in relation to their works. Congress concluded that existing U.S. laws protected authors' rights to a degree sufficient to allow the United States to sign the international agreement.

The laws that affect authors' moral rights include the Lanham Act, various state statutes, and common law principles such as libel, defamation, misrepresentation, and unfair competition.

In 1990 Congress passed the "Visual Artists' Rights Act of 1990."[25] This act protects original works in single copies and limited editions by preventing any intentional distortion, mutilation, or other modification that would prejudice an author's reputation. The Act also prevents any intentional or gross negligence that would result in the destruction of a work of recognized stature.

Myth 18: When copyright laws conflict with the first amendment's guarantee of freedom of speech, the copyright law is invalid.

The courts have generally held that in most instances there can be no conflict between free speech and the copyright law.[26] This is largely because the copyright law protects the expression, not the idea. Ideas can be expressed in innumerable ways without copying someone else's particular expression. For example, if someone wanted to express their idea about a mouse, they could do so without copying Disney's idea of Mickey Mouse.

On the other hand, the courts have acknowledged some rare instances in which there have been conflicts. In a famous case[27], *Life Magazine* sued a historian for copying frames of the Zapruder films of the assassination of John F. Kennedy. The court ruled that the "public interest in having the fullest information available on the murder of President Kennedy" justified the copying. This is a rare exception, however, and is limited to graphic expression of newsworthy events. It is difficult to imagine a situation where the First Amendment and the copyright law would conflict in a case involving a library's usual activities.

Endnotes

1. 17 U.S.C. §109(a) reads: . . . the owner of a particular copy or phonorecord lawfully made under this title, or any person authorized by such owner, is entitled, without the authority of the copyright owner, to sell, or otherwise dispose of the possession of the copy or phonorecord.
.2. See Appendix B for the text and where to affix the warning.
3. 17 U.S.C. §108(g)(2).
4. 17 U.S.C. §109(b) also provides that a library or its employees while performing their jobs can also project a single image of it one at a time and at the same place where it is being exhibited. The subsection reads: ". . . the owner of a particular copy lawfully made under this title, or any person authorized by such owner, is entitled, without the authority of the copyright owner, to display that copy publicly, either directly or by the projection of no more than one image at a time, to viewers present at the place where the copy is located.".
5. House Report (Judiciary Committee) No. 94-1476, September 3, 1976 [To accompany S.22], pp. 79-80.
6. House Report 94-1476, p.80.
7. A Library could display a work which was first purchased by one library and then "lent" to another library. The key here is that the work must be first purchased from the copyright owner by someone. This is where the term "first sale doctrine" derives from.
8. 17 U.S.C. §105.
9. According to House Report No. 94-1476, p. 59, the copyright law: ". . . deliberately avoids making any sort of outright, unqualified prohibition against copyright in works prepared under Government contract or grant. There may well be cases where it would be in the public interest to deny copyright in writings generated by Government research contracts and the like. . . ."
10. U.S. Government publications can be copyrighted if created in a country that copyrights the works of its own government. Or as House Report 94-1476, p.59 states: "The prohibition on copyright protection for United States Government works is not intended to have any effect on protection of those works abroad. Works of governments of most other countries are copyrighted. There are no valid policy reasons for denying

such protection to the United States Government works in foreign countries. . . ."

11. Private works published by the U.S. Government can be copyrighted if eligible. Publication by the federal government does not affect their copyright status. See House Report No. 94-1476, p.60.

12. NTIS copyrights are limited to 5 years. House Report No. 94-1476, p.60.

13. Works of employees of the U.S. Postal Service can be copyrighted. House Report No. 94-1476, p.60.

14. 17 U.S.C. §102(b).

15. 37 CFR §202.1.

16. 17 U.S.C. §113(a) states: ". . . the exclusive right to reproduce a copyrighted pictorial, graphic, or sculptural work in copies . . . includes the right to reproduce the work in or on any kind of article, whether useful or otherwise."

17. According to 17 U.S.C. §120: "The copyright in an architectural work that has been constructed does not include the right to prevent the making, distribution, or public display of pictures, paintings, photographs, or other pictorial representations of the work, if the building in which the work is embodied is located in or ordinarily visible from a public place." This section was added on December 1, 1990 and is applicable to architectural work created on or after December 1, 1990. There are other restrictions.

18. According to House Report No. 94-1476, p.55: "The Committee does not regard the design of typefaces . . . to be copyrightable."

19. *Atascadero State Hospital* v. *Scanlon*, 473 U.S. 234 (1985).

20. 17 U.S.C. §511, P.L. 101-553, 104 Stat. 2749 (November 15, 1990). See House Report (Judiciary Committee) No. 101-282(I), October 13, 1989 [To accompany H.R. 3045], p.1 for discussion of purpose. The text of this act appears in Appendix D.

21. In House Report 94-1476 the Judiciary Committee states on page 61: "As under the present law, a copyrighted work would be infringed by reproducing it in whole or in any substantial part, and by duplicating it exactly or by imitation or simulation. *Wide departures or variations from the copyrighted work would still be an infringement as long as the author's 'expressions' rather than merely the author's 'ideas' are taken* [emphasis added]."

22. For example, Learned Hand's abstraction test (45 F.2d at 121). In this test you make general statements about a work until you come to a point where it can no longer be protected. For example, if all you are copying is the idea of a story about two people in love when their gangs are at war with each other, you are probably not infringing on *West Side Story*.

23. According to 17 U.S.C. § 107: "In determining whether the use made of a work in any particular case is a fair use the factors to be considered shall include—

    1. the purpose and character of use, including whether such use is of a commercial nature or is for nonprofit educational purposes;

2. the nature of the copyrighted work;

3. the amount and substantiality of the portion used in relation to the copyrighted work as a whole ;

4. the effect of use upon potential market or value of the copyrighted work."

24. 17 U.S.C. §103(b).

25. Pub. L. 101-650, 104 Stat. 5128, 5133 (December 1, 1990).

26. *Sid & Marty Krofft Television* v. *McDonald's Corporation*, 562 F.2d 1157, 1171 (1977).

27. *Time, Inc.* v. *Bernard Geis Associates*, 293 F.Supp. 130 (1968). See discussion in *Sid & Marty Krofft Television* v. *McDonald's Corporation*, 562 F.2d at 1171 (1977).

2
Historical and Legal Background

- *What purpose is the copyright law meant to serve?*

- *Historically, how has this purpose evolved?*

- *How have libraries played a role in the history of copyright laws?*

Of all the laws that affect libraries, the copyright law is one of the most pervasive and profound in its impact. Virtually every library operation—both internal and with other libraries—is affected in some way by its dictates. From photocopying a volume for preservation to faxing a journal article to respond to a patron's request, libraries must continually be concerned with avoiding copyright infringement. Yet despite its importance to librarians, the copyright law remains somewhat of a mystery. Librarians know they must comply but may not understand why.

To understand the purpose and reason for having a copyright law—in fact, to understand the copyright law itself—we need to see how the copyright law came about. Like most laws, copyright evolved gradually into what it is today.

THREE KEY FACTORS

There are three important things to remember about the evolution of the copyright law:

1. Copyright has always been a grant of exclusive rights. The owner of a copyright is given rights that go far beyond the rights granted to owners of other types of property.[1] For example, a copyright owner can prevent anyone from changing his or her original work and then selling it without permission. A homeowner, on the other hand, could improve a home and resell it at any time without any permission from the original builder.
2. There is some significant benefit gained in exchange for the grant of these exclusive rights to a copyright owner. For example, copyrights were at first granted by the British Crown as a means of enforcing censorship and securing the throne's control over the presses.
3. All copyright legislation must balance these benefits against each other. Ultimately the benefits to the grantor—whether that is the Crown or the general public—must far outweigh those to the individual copyright owner.

Libraries have been and will continue to be a major force in shaping copyright legislation. Without the tremendous growth of the public library, there would have been no real need for copyright laws. This explains why the growth of libraries so closely parallels the development of the copyright law.

PRIOR TO THE PRINTING PRESS

Did copyright laws exist before the invention of the printing press? This question is best answered by looking at the libraries that were available to the public in the classical world and the functions they served.

Early libraries were largely private collections of rare, one-of-a-kind items—clay tablets in Babylon and papyrus rolls in the temple libraries of Egypt. There was no need for a copyright law because access to information was limited and the physical works were carefully guarded. Very few, if any, copies could be made. Authors were also members of a leisure class whose status rested on limiting access to knowledge.

Libraries in ancient Greece were largely for preserving past works. The tradition of passing stories orally from one generation to another, with each adding its own contributions, did not require any regulations governing monetary or proprietary rewards—only careful preservation. In fact, the first public library was established in 330 B.C., largely to house and preserve accurate copies of the works of Greek dramatists. At the Library at Alexandria, the works of all Greek authors were carefully collected, compiled, and recopied.

Public libraries in Rome, however, served more than a preservation function. Rome libraries began with collections taken from conquered nations and built upon them. Libraries came to be used for both research and recreation and created an interest in new works. For the first time in the ancient world, authors could sell copies of their own works or those of their servants. This brief period when authors received compensation for their works, however, did not continue.

Libraries in the Middle Ages carefully preserved manuscripts in monasteries. Monks copied and illuminated them. In the medieval scriptorium, a complex set of rules existed to determine:

- what works could or could not be copied
- by whom they could be copied
- for whom they could be copied.

In fact, in what must have been the first copyright case, a copy of a manuscript made without its owner's consent was returned to its original owner, with the court noting, "To every cow her calf."

In short, before the invention of the printing press and the ability to produce large numbers of copies, property rights to books generally belonged to the possessor, not the creator, except for that brief period in ancient Rome.

THE PRINTING PRESS

With the invention of the printing press in 1455, libraries began to increase in size and number as books became less expensive and more available. National libraries were established in many countries, and the interest in books and literary works increased. Then as now, libraries were dedicated to the improvement of human knowledge and the promotion of literacy and information access. The property rights to books, however, passed to the printers and booksellers.

In England, authors were no longer allowed to print and market their own works. In fact, only members of a specific guild of printers and booksellers, the Stationers' Company, were given the right by the Crown to print and sell books. All others were barred from doing so. Anyone who failed to have their presses certified risked their destruction and a year's imprisonment. The penalty for even selling non-approved works was three months' imprisonment.

With a guaranteed monopoly, members of the Stationers' Company purchased from authors the perpetual copyright of their books, usually for a single one-time fee. The bookseller became the proprietor of the book's "copy-right" and had the sole right to print. The bookseller could resell the right or continue to profit from the sale of the books. Courts considered the right's value in awarding judgments. Copyrights were part of a bookseller's estate which he or she could bequeath to an heir.

Authors received no residuals and were not entitled to share in the continuing profit and success of their own works. Being forced to go to only one guild and to sell their works when they were least valuable, authors received only a fraction of what their works were worth, and many authors found themselves in a destitute condition.

Why did this happen? Why did the British government create and sanction such a process? The monarchy's principal reason for creating this monopoly was to retain control of the new printing industry. The Stationers' Company was created by Henry VIII and chartered under Queen Mary in 1556 for the purpose of stopping the printing of subversive or heretic works. Registered members of the Stationers' Company guaranteed and certified that all works published by them passed the censors and contained no insurrectionary material. As stated by a judge in 1769: "By the charter of Queen Mary, the Company of Stationers were made a kind of literary constable, to seize all books that were printed contrary to the statute."

The bylaws of the Stationers' Company required members to record the title of the book in the "Register-Book" of the Stationers' Company and to pay a fee for any book they printed. Those who did not pay this fee or those who printed books registered and recorded by other members were subject to fines, confiscation, or even imprisonment. All these rights were enforced by a court that acted without a jury and without controls, the Court of the Star Chamber. This system gave the monarchy absolute control over publishing.

The decrees of the Star Chamber, however, particularly those supporting the Crown over Parliament in church matters, resulted in the court's abolition in 1641 by the Long Parliament. All of its regulations, including those regulating printing, were thus repealed. Without controls on printing, particularly after such a long period of control, piracy flourished.

The abuses that followed resulted in the passage of a new licensing act in 1643. This act once again required registration with the Stationers' Company. Penalties under the Act included forfeiture of copies to the owner. Later, fines were levied against violators.

A new requirement was also introduced, one that survives even today and has proven invaluable to the new national library collections. This was the requirement that a work be deposited. The primary reason for deposit was to prevent fraud. In case of infringement, the copy of record would be the one on deposit. In this way, the courts could always be assured of having an unaltered copy to which to refer. The 1643 act required a copy to be deposited at the King's Library and at each of the universities. When these reform acts finally expired in 1694, the statutory penalties lapsed and piracy once again flourished in England.

THE FIRST COPYRIGHT STATUTE

It was against this backdrop that in 1710 the famous Statute of Queen Anne was passed. This statute remains the foundation of copyright law in England and the United States today.

The full title of the act was "A Bill for the Encouragement of Learning, by Vesting the Copies of Printed Books in the Authors or Purchasers of Such Copies, during the Times therein mentioned" and it took effect on April 10, 1710. The act began with the following statement of purpose:

> Whereas Printers, Booksellers, and other Persons have of late frequently taken the Liberty of printing, reprinting, and publishing or causing to be printed, reprinted, and published books, and other Writings, without Consent of the Authors or Proprietors of such Books and writings, to their great Detriment, and too often to the Ruin of them and their Families: preventing therefore such Practices for the future, and for the Encourage-ment of learned men to compose and write useful Books, may it please Your Majesty, that it may be enacted. . . .

The statute was the first time in history that the rights of an author were explicitly acknowledged. Authors were to have the sole right of printing their works for a set period of time:

· for existing works—21 years from the effective date of the act
· for works not yet printed—14 years and an additional 14 years if the author was still alive at the end of the first term.

Books could not be exported without the written consent of the author or owner of the printing rights. More significantly, however, the penalty for selling counterfeit copies was forfeiture and a then substantial fine of one "peny" per page.

The statute also set forth several preconditions that had to be met before an infringement suit could be brought. The book had to be entered in the register book of the Stationers' Company, and the suit had to be brought within three months of the offense. The deposit requirement was once again introduced, and the number of required copies increased to nine. The statute also provided for a subtle form of price control. If the asking price of a book was too high, the Queen's officers could direct that it be lowered.

When the first term granted in the 1710 act expired in 1731, a battle ensured over the rights to copyright. Owners of titles in the Register of the Stationers' Company claimed that they still had a copyright in perpetuity. After all, they had purchased the "copyrights" believing that they would not be limited in duration. Other booksellers claimed that the copyright had lapsed according to the Statute of Queen Anne.

In *Millar v. Taylor* (1769), the courts held that the perpetual rights continued despite the limitations imposed in the Statute of Queen Anne, but in a subsequent case, *Donaldson v. Beckett* (1774), the House of Lords reversed the earlier decision by the narrow margin of six to five. That one swing vote was significant because it established that an author had two rights: 1) prior to publication, an author had the sole right to the work in perpetuity, but; 2) once published, the author's rights were limited to the term set by the statute.

SIGNIFICANCE

The significance of the events that led to the passage of the first copyright law was the recognition that the best means of encouraging creativity was to grant authors the right to the fruits of their labor. The attempt to deprive authors of these rights and control a new technology failed and proved the futility of such efforts.

Other by-products of these early laws continue to be important in the copyright law today:

Registration: While registration began as a means of controlling what was printed and preserving the monopoly of the Stationers' Company, it serves today to provide a legal record of ownership. Today registration is a prerequisite to bringing an infringement suit in the United States.

Deposit: Even today, the deposit requirement must be fulfilled before an infringement suit can be brought, and deposit remains one of the principal ways the Library of Congress acquires new titles.

Term of copyright: The use of multiples of 14 years survived in the United States until 1976.

Pre-publication rights of authors: The perpetual rights of authors to their creative works before publication and the changes made to those rights after publication existed right up to 1976, when a new copyright law became effective in the United States. What began as a means of depriving authors of their rights to profit from their labors came to serve as protection for authors' unpublished manuscripts until they were protected by a new statute.

Manufacturing Clause: The Statute of Queen Anne was limited to British writers. The status of works printed in other countries was yet to be determined. In the United States, the requirement that a work be printed in the United States before it was given the protection of U.S. laws died hard and existed in some form right into the 20th century.

One provision that did not last very long was price control. The provision calling for a price rollback if too much was asked for a copy of a book was repealed in England in 1739.

The most significant and lasting effect of the Statute of Queen Anne was the recognition that, as stated by an English judge in 1769:

> It is wise in any state to encourage letters, and the painful researches of learned men. The easiest and most equal way of doing it, is by securing to them the property of their own works.

FURTHER DEVELOPMENTS

In England, the copyright law was extended beyond books and literary works specified in the Statute of Queen Anne. In 1734, it was extended to engravings and prints, in 1798 to sculpture, in 1833 to dramatic works, in 1835 to lectures, in 1842 to manufacturing designs and in 1862 to paintings, drawings, and photographs.

Authors were also relieved of many of the formal requirements for obtaining a copyright. In 1814, authors were no longer required to deposit copies in 11 libraries, except upon demand. In 1836, this number was reduced to five.

The period of copyright was also extended. The Literary Copyright Act of 1842 made the period the life of the author plus 7 years, or a term of 42 years, whichever was longer.

Endnotes

1. Copyrights are part of an area of the law known as "intellectual property," which also includes patents and trademarks.

3
Copyright Law in the United States

- *What is the source of the U.S. copyright law?*

- *How did the U.S. copyright law evolve into its present form?*

- *In what ways does the current copyright law in the United States affect libraries?*

HISTORY

The English Statute of Queen Anne formed the basis for copyright law in America. Colonial America was very familiar with the events that led to the statute's passage, and its provisions continued to serve as a model even after separation from England. It was unquestioned in America that the best means of advancing the arts and sciences was to recognize authors' rights to their own creations.

In May 1783, the Continental Congress recommended to the states that they pass their own copyright laws. Like the Statute of Queen Anne, the term of copyright protection was generally 14 years with another 14-year extension. Some even contained the provision similar to the original English statute relating to price controls, which had been repealed in England in 1739. Ultimately, all the states except Delaware adopted their own copyright laws.

A copyright clause was part of the U.S. Constitution when it was adopted in 1787. Article I, Section 8, Clause 8 of the U.S. Constitution reads:

To promote the progress of science and the useful arts, by securing for
limited time to authors and inventors the exclusive right to their respective writings and discoveries.

There is no evidence of any disagreement among the drafters of
the Constitution over this clause. In *The Federalist Papers* it was
noted that this clause could "scarcely be questioned" and the "public
good fully coincides in both cases with the claims of the individual"
(#43).

Copyright Law of 1790

As one of its first acts in 1790, the new U.S. Congress passed a
national copyright law. This first U.S. copyright law was entitled:
"An act for the encouragement of learning, by securing the copies of
maps, charts, and books, to the authors and proprietors of such
copies, during the time therein mentioned." The law granted authors
who were citizens or residents copyright[1] in books, maps, and charts
for 14 years with renewal for 14 years more if the author was living at
expiration of the first term. Procedures for acquiring a copyright
were:

1. Before publication, a printed copy of the title of a map, chart, book, or
   books was deposited in the clerk's office of the District Court where the
   author or proprietor resided.
2. The clerk of the court recorded the title.
3. Within two months, a copy of that record was to be published in one or
   more newspapers for a space of four weeks.
4. Within six months, a copy was to be deposited with the U.S. Secretary
   of State.

Failure to complete these procedures in the time specified and in
the manner required would result in loss of copyright. The penalties
for infringement were forfeiture and a fine of 50 cents for each sheet
found. Half of the fine went to the U.S. government. The infringement
suit had to be started within one year after the infringement occurred. The first U.S. copyright law made no provisions for copyrighting
foreign works written by non-citizens or non-residents of the U.S.
except to permit their importation into or reprinting or publishing in
the United States.

Copyright Law of 1831

The first major revision of the copyright law occurred in 1831.[2] A major revision repeals all previous editions as well as effecting significant changes in a law.

Musical compositions, prints and engravings were added to the list of items that could be copyrighted.[3] The first term of copyright was increased from 14 to 28 years. If the author, or his or her spouse or children, were still alive at the end of the 28 years and were still citizens or residents of the United States, the copyright could be renewed for 14 more years. Thus, the maximum number of years that copyright protection could be continued under this act was 42.

Procedures for acquiring a copyright were:

1. Before publication, a printed copy of the title of the book or books, map, chart, musical composition, print, cut, or engraving had to be deposited in the clerk's office of the District Court of the district where the author or proprietor resided.
2. The clerk of the court had to record the title.
3. Within three months after publication, a copy of that work had to be delivered to the clerk of the district court.
4. At least once a year, the clerk of the court had to send to the Secretary of State a certified list of all copies deposited.

For the first time, a copyright notice had to be printed in the work itself in order to secure a copyright. For a book, the notice had to appear on the title page or on the page immediately following it. For a map, chart, musical composition, print, cut, or engraving the notice was required on the face or frontispiece. The notice read: "Entered according to act of Congress, in the year ____ , by A.B., in the clerk's office of the district court of _____."[4]

Penalties for infringement included forfeiture and a fine of 50 cents per sheet for books and one dollar per sheet for other works. In addition, the infringer was liable for all damages that resulted from the injury. Copyright owners could also obtain injunctions to prevent violation of their rights. All actions were required to be brought within two years of the infringement.

Copyright Law of 1870

The next major revision occurred in 1870. Paintings, drawings, chromos, statues, statuaries, and models or designs intended to be perfected as works of fine art were added to the list of items that could be copyrighted. Also added was the exclusive right to publicly perform dramatic compositions. Authors could also reserve the right to dramatize or translate their own works.[5]

Procedures for acquiring a copyright were:

1. Before publication, a printed copy of the title of the book or other article, or a description of the painting, drawing, chromo, statue, statuary, or model or design for a work of the fine arts had to be deposited in the mail, addressed to the librarian of Congress.
2. Within ten days after publication, two complete printed copies of the best edition of a book or article—or, in the case of a painting, drawing, statue, statuary, model, or design, a photograph—had to be deposited in the mail, addressed to the librarian of Congress. Books and articles for deposit could be sent postage-free.
3. No action for infringement could be brought unless a notice of copyright[6] was inserted on the title page or the page immediately following in the case of a book or on the face or front of the other works.

Publications previously sent to the Department of the Interior or to the clerks of the district courts were to be sent to the librarian of Congress along with all records. A penalty of $100 and forfeiture was provided for anyone who inserted a copyright notice and had not obtained a copyright. The penalty for infringing a copyright included forfeiture, fines, and damages.

Copyright Law of 1909

The next major revision of U.S. copyright law occurred in 1909. This revision remained in effect until 1978.

The total number of years that copyright protection was available increased to a total of 56 (Section 24 of the Act). The manufacturing clause continued and expanded to require binding and typesetting as well as printing within the United States (Section 16). Procedures for acquiring a copyright were:

1. Notice of copyright had to be affixed to each copy published or offered for sale in the United States (Section 10 of the Act). The notice of copyright was generally either the word "Copyright," "Copr.," or © followed by the name of the copyright owner and the year in which the copyright was secured (Section 17). Failure to include the notice resulted in loss of copyright forever.
2. Registration (Section 11) and deposit of two complete copies of the best edition with the Register of Copyrights (Section 13). No action for infringement could be maintained unless deposit and registration have been complied with. Failure to deposit also could result in a fine and voiding of copyright (Section 14).

Copyright consisted of the exclusive right:[7]

- to print, reprint, publish, copy, and vend
- to translate or make other versions

- to deliver, read, or present in public for profit if it be a lecture, sermon, address or similar production, or other nondramatic literary work
- to perform or represent publicly if it be a drama
- to perform publicly for profit if it be a musical composition.

Copyrighted works were classified into 13 categories for registration purposes:

- books, including composite and cyclopedic works, directories, gazetteers, and other compilations
- periodicals, including newspapers
- lectures, sermons, addresses (prepared for oral delivery)
- dramatic or dramatico-musical compositions
- musical compositions
- maps
- works of arts; models or designs for works of arts
- reproductions of a work of art
- drawings or plastic works of a scientific or technical character
- photographs
- prints and pictorial illustrations including prints or labels used for articles of merchandise
- motion-picture photoplays
- motion pictures other than photoplays.

Copyright also began with publication, creating a distinction pre- and post-publication. After publication, the federal copyright provided protection. Prior to publication, authors had to depend on state law. As in England, an author or his heirs had the sole right to an unpublished work in perpetuity (Section 2). Once published, it fell under the maximum federal protection of 56 years.

The Copyright Law of 1909 codified the "first sale doctrine" (Section 27). Under this doctrine, once a library has acquired a lawful copy, it may lend that particular copy, imposing whatever conditions it chooses to impose. It can even resell that copy.

Copyright Law of 1976

Each new revision of the copyright law:

- added to the list of creative works that can be copyrighted (see Table 1 at the end of this chapter)
- increased the length of copyright protection (see Table 2 at the end of this chapter)
- made procedures for acquiring a copyright less cumbersome (see Table 3 at the end of this chapter)

However impressive these reforms may seem, they did not keep pace with developments occurring in English copyright law and those happening in other countries.

Among the significant differences between U.S. copyright law and those happening in other countries were:

- *Term of copyright protection.* In 1842, the term of copyright protection in England was already the life of the author plus 7 years. In that same year in America, it was only 28 years with a 14-year renewal.
- *International copyright protection.* The U.S. copyright law did not offer protection to anyone but U.S. citizens and residents until 1891. An international copyright law had been passed in England in 1838. In 1885, most of the major nations of the world held a diplomatic conference resulting in the Berne Convention. Signers agreed they would recognize each other's copyrights and would make essential changes to bring their copyright laws up to a high international standard. This became effective in 1887, but the United States was not a signatory to this convention because it could not meet this standard.
- *Manufacturing clause.* Another major difference between U.S. copyright law and that of other major countries was the United States' long retention of the "manufacturing clause." The clause actually originated in England in 1534. The clause made obtaining a U.S. copyright contingent upon printing in the United States. This clause survived until 1986 and is the reason for the notice printed in Amerian books that reads, "Printed in the United States."

The purpose of this next revision of the copyright law was to bring the United States more in line with the copyright laws of other countries and to begin making the changes necessary for the United States to sign the Berne Convention. The revision was passed in 1976 and became effective on January 1, 1978. This is the current copyright law in the United States together with its subsequent amendments.

The term of copyright protection was extended from the maximum length of 56 years to the more internationally recognized term of the life of the author plus 50 years. For works made for hire, and for anonymous and pseudonymous works, the duration of copyright protection is 75 years from publication or 100 years from creation, whichever is shorter.

The act also eliminated the distinction between published and unpublished work, fixing copyright by the moment of creation rather than the date of publication. The authors of unpublished manuscripts written after January 1, 1978, no longer retained their common law rights in perpetuity. Like other authors, their term of copyright is the same as that of published authors—life plus fifty years.

The act also did not make the failure to include a copyright notice on the verso (reverse side) of the title page a fatal mistake as it was previously. This brought the U.S. law closer to the internationally accepted practice of recognizing copyright without a notice affixed. In addition, the act expanded the list of works that could be copyrighted. Under this new law, copyright was extended to protect all "original works of authorship" that are fixed in a tangible medium. They can be communicated through a machine or device. There are now eight categories of copyrightable works:

- literary works
- musical works, including any accompanying words
- dramatic works, including any accompanying music
- pantomimes and choreographic works
- pictorial, graphic, and sculptural works
- motion pictures and other audiovisual works
- sound recordings
- architectural works.

These categories are not viewed as exclusive. Computer programs, for example, are registrable as "literary works." Maps and architectural plans are registrable as "pictorial, graphic, and sculptural works."

The act incorporated the judicially created doctrine of fair use as part of the statute. Fair use allows copying of copyrighted works under specific limited conditions. Libraries and archives also were given some exclusive rights of their own under Section 108 of the act.

Subsequent Amendments

The 1976 act has been amended several times since its enactment. The changes that most affect libraries are:

- *Computer software.* In 1980, an important addition was made to the list of exceptions to an author's exclusive rights. Copying of computer software is not an infringement if: 1) the copy is created as an essential step in using the program, or; 2) it is done for archival purposes only and the copy is destroyed if the software is no longer owned.[8]
- *Phonorecords and computer software rentals.* Phonorecords were eliminated from the first sale doctrine in 1984[9] and computer software in 1990.[10] Under these changes, particular copies of phonorecords and computer programs (including any tapes and disks) cannot be rented, leased or lent either for direct or indirect commercial gain. Nonprofit lending by nonprofit libraries and educational institutions is exempt. A warning of copyright must be affixed to the package containing the

computer program. Anyone else who distributes a phonorecord or a copy of computer software in violation of these acts is an infringer, subject to criminal penalties. No later than December 1, 1993, the Register of Copyrights, after consultation with representatives of copyright owners and librarians, shall submit to Congress a report stating whether the act has achieved its intended purpose while allowing nonprofit libraries to fulfill their functions.

- *Berne Implementation Act.* In 1988, the significant changes needed to make it possible for the U.S. to sign the Berne Convention were made to U.S. copyright law. These changes have direct impact on libraries. One of the most significant changes for libraries was the elimination of the copyright notice as a requirement for copyright. This means a work created after March 1, 1989, may not have a copyright notice, yet it may still be copyrighted. This makes it more difficult for librarians to identify copyrighted works. Other changes include: deposit in the Library of Congress no longer affects the copyright status of a work, but deposit is still mandatory; and failure to deposit is still subject to fine. Registration of a copyrighted work is necessary before it is possible to bring an infringement suit.
- *Copyright Remedy Clarification Act.*[11] In 1990, Congress passed this act making it clear that states and local governments can be sued in federal court for copyright infringements and are liable for money damages. This means that public libraries are definitely liable for copyright infringements.
- *Moral Rights.* In 1990, Congress passed the "Visual Artists Rights Act of 1990."[12] This act protects original works in single copies and limited editions by preventing any intentional distortion, mutilation, or other modification of the work that could damage an author's reputation. The act also prevents any intentional or gross negligence that would result in destruction of a work of recognized stature.

THE CURRENT LAW

The basis for the current copyright law in the United States is the same as it has been for all of its earlier version—the copyright clause of the U.S. Constitution, Article I, Section 8, Clause 8:

To promote the progress of science and the useful arts, by securing for limited time to authors and inventors the exclusive right to their respective writings and discoveries.

What can be copyrighted? The copyright clause uses the terms "authors" and "their respective writings." There are still two basic requirements for copyright protection:

- originality (an author is, after all, someone who creates something original)
- fixation in a tangible medium (writings).

Thus, under the current copyright law of the United States, copyright protection subsists in "original works of authorship." This is clearly not intended to mean that a work must be novel or ingenious or have any aesthetic merit to receive copyright protection. To be copyrighted a work need only be "original" to its creator, whether it has existed before or not. Unlike a patent, there is no search conducted to determine if a similar work had been created before, and to bring an infringement action, it has to be shown that a work has been copied from another.

The second fundamental requirement is that the work be "fixed in a tangible medium of expression." After all the "Writings" in the copyright clause are not just ideas—they are actually written down on a physical object. Authors are, however, always finding new media, including electronic media, sound, and video systems. To prevent freezing what can be copyrighted at the current stage of technology, the new law added the phrase "now known or later developed." According to the new law, a "tangible medium" is something "from which they (author's writings) can be perceived, reproduced, or otherwise communicated, either directly or with the aid of a machine or device."[13]

What Cannot Be Copyrighted?

As important as it is to know what can be copyrighted, it is perhaps more important to know what cannot be, especially now that a copyright notice is not required for a work to be copyrighted. First of all, copyright protection does not extend to any:

> . . . idea, procedure, process, system, method of operation, concept, principle, or discovery, regardless of the form in which it is described, explained, illustrated, or embodied in such work.[14]

These exceptions also derive from the copyright clause of the Constitution. If an idea were given copyright protection, it would bar any other works based upon that idea, and this would clearly not advance the arts and sciences.

Exclusive Rights

Under current U.S. law, copyright owners have the exclusive right to:

- *reproduce* their copyrighted work
- prepare *derivative* works based upon their copyrighted work
- *distribute* copies to the public
- *perform* their copyrighted work publicly
- *display* their copyrighted work publicly.

It is illegal under federal law for anyone to violate any of these rights, but there are significant limitations to them. If it were not for these exceptions, no one could photocopy, perform, or display a copyrighted work in any library in the United States without violating the law.

Limitations on Copyright

Three limitations that are of particular interest to libraries are first sale doctrine, fair use and the special rights granted specifically to libraries and archives.

1. First Sale Doctrine.[15] Once a library has purchased (or has purchased for them) any print item (book, periodical, pamphlet, etc.), phonorecord (recording), or piece of computer software, the library may lend that legally obtained copy without the permission of the copyright owner. For books and other print matter, the library may lend the original as many times as needed. In addition, it may make its own lending rules concerning the print material. There are some procedures that must be complied with concerning phonorecords and computer programs before they can be lent, including the affixing of a copyright warning notice. (See Appendix B.)

Once a copyright owner has sold a copy of a printed work, the person to whom the copy is sold is entitled to dispose of it by sale, rental, lease, or other means. There are limitations, however, on phonorecords and computer programs.[16] These cannot be rented, leased, or lent for direct or indirect commercial gain. Any person so doing is an infringer, subject to criminal penalties. The only exceptions are nonprofit libraries or nonprofit educational institutions engaged in nonprofit lending. In the case of software, nonprofit libraries must affix to the package containing the software a warning of copyright.

2. Fair use. Fair use was created by the courts and was incorporated into the copyright statute as Section 107. Fair use is available for purposes such as teaching, scholarship, or research. In determining whether copying of a work is fair use, there are four factors to consider:

1. The purpose and character of the use, including whether such use is of a commercial nature or is for nonprofit educational purposes.
2. The nature of the copyrighted work.
3. The amount and substantiality of the portion used in relation to the copyrighted work as a whole.
4. The effect of the use upon the potential market for or value of the copyrighted work.

Fair use is based on the concept of reasonableness, and these four standards are to be considered and weighed together.

Factor 1, the purpose and character of the use, looks at whether the copying is being done for commercial gain, nonprofit research, or educational purposes. Just because copies are being made for educational purposes without monetary gain, however, this does not automatically qualify as fair use. The other factors must also be weighed.

Factor 2 considers the nature of the copyrighted work. The copying of factual works is more likely to be deemed fair use than the copying of fiction, since there is presumably a greater need to disseminate information "to advance human knowledge."[17] Some fields such as history, science, medicine, and law depend on references to previous works and must quote and cite them frequently.

Factor 3 is not just a quantitative measure. Even if only one sentence is taken from a large work, if that sentence contains the essence or heart of a work, then copying it may not qualify as fair use.

Factor 4 looks at the effect the copying has on the potential market for the original work and weighs the injury caused by such copying. In such cases, the courts may also look to see if copying is done only to avoid doing original research.

Consider the court's analysis in one of the most famous library photocopying cases, *Williams & Wilkins Co.* v. *United States.*[18] In this case, which occurred while Congress was working on the Copyright Law of 1976, a major publisher of medical journals sued a federal medical research organization and its library for copyright infringement of four of its journals. The library photocopied articles from the medical journals at the request of researchers and medical practitioners and made interlibrary loans. The copying was massive, involving 93,000 articles in 1970 alone. The library restricted copying, however, on individual requests to a single copy of a single article and to articles of less than 50 pages. Interlibrary loans were made only if the article was at least five years old or was not from one of the 100 journals considered to be widely available.[19]

The analysis of this case is helpful in understanding "fair use."

1. The court noted that the copying was for non-commercial use and was for a limited class of requesters.
2. The court noted that the copying was from two areas of research—science and education—that depended highly upon past works.
3. The court noted that the requests normally were limited to single articles of 50 pages or less. Even though the copy was of an entire article, it could be considered a discreet whole, not the entire journal.
4. The court found the effect on the market to be minimal. The medical publisher failed to show that it had been substantially harmed by the library's practices.

The court concluded that the copying was fair use.

In a case involving a motion picture which was based upon a copyrighted story, the court ruled quite differently. The taking does not fall within the purposes "such as criticism, comment, news reporting, teaching (including multiple copies for classroom use), scholarship, or research." Factor 1: the copying was for commercial use. Factor 2: the work taken was a creative product, not a factual work. Factor 3: it was determined that essentially the heart of the book was taken although only 20% of it was used. Factor 4: the court determined that the release of the film impinged on the ability to market new versions of the story. The U.S. Supreme Court[20] agreed with the lower court decision: All four factors point to copyright infringement. This case is a classic example of an unfair use: a commercial use of a fictional story that adversely affects the story owner's adaptation rights.

3. Library Privileges. The third limitation on copyright under the current law is the granting of special rights to libraries, set forth under Section 108 of the act. These rights are the result of a massive lobbying effort by library organizations. Under this Section, libraries can reproduce and distribute copies for:

- *Archival reproduction.* Unpublished work may be copied in its original or facsimile format solely for the purposes of preservation and security. Copies can also be made for the purpose of depositing a copy in another library or archive if the copy is currently in the collection of the first library or archive. Only unpublished works can be copied, but the right to copy extends to any type of work, including photographs, motion pictures, and sound recordings. Under this exemption, for example, a library could microfilm a manuscript but could not reproduce the work in machine-readable language for computer storage.
- *Replacement of damaged copies.* A published work may be copied in its

original or facsimile format solely for the purpose of replacement of a copy or phonorecord that is damaged, deteriorating, lost, or stolen if the library or archive has, after a reasonable effort, determined that an unused replacement cannot be obtained at a fair price. The search for a reasonably priced replacement will vary with circumstances but must include commonly known trade sources in the United States, and in normal situations also the publisher or other copyright owner, or an authorized copy service. The owner can be located from the address listed in the copyright registration.

- *Articles and small excerpts.* Libraries can copy and distribute a copy of not more than one article or other contribution from a copyrighted collection or periodical issue, or a copy or phonorecord of a small part of any other copyrighted work. The copy or phonorecord may be made by the library where the user makes the request or by another library as part of an interlibrary loan. It is further required that the copy become the property of the user, that the library or archives be unaware of any purpose for the copy other than private study, scholarship, or research; and that the library or archives display prominently at the place where reproduction requests are accepted, and include on its order forms, a warning about copyright regulations in accordance with those required by the Register of Copyrights.

- *Out-of-print works.* Libraries can copy or distribute a copy or phonorecord of an entire out-of-print work under certain circumstances if it has been established that a copy cannot be obtained at a fair price. The copy may be made by the library where the user makes the request or by another library as part of an interlibrary loan. The scope and nature of a reasonable investigation to determine that an unused copy cannot be obtained will vary according to the circumstances of each particular situation. It will always require recourse to commonly known trade sources in the United States, and in normal situations also to the publisher or other copyright owner (if the owner can be located at the address listed in the copyright registration), or to an authorized reproducing service. It is further required that the copy become the property of the user; that the library or archives be unaware of any purpose for the copy other than private study, scholarship, or research; and that the library or archives display prominently at the place where reproduction requests are accepted, and include on its order forms, a warning about copyright regulations (in accordance with those required by the Register of Copyrights).

- *General Exemptions.* Libraries and archives are specifically exempted from liability for the unsupervised use of photocopiers provided that they post a notice stating that the making of copies may be subject to the copyright law. Libraries may also make off-the-air videotape recordings of daily network newscasts for limited distribution to scholars and researchers for use in research purposes. Contractual obligations are not overridden by any provisions of the copyright act.

- *Multiple Copies and Systematic Reproduction.* The rights granted under this Section apply *only* to the "isolated and unrelated reproduction of a single copy or phonorecord of the same material on separate occasions."
- *Interlibrary Loan Arrangements.* Nothing prevents a libraries or archives from participating in interlibrary arrangements so long as the purpose or effect of the arrangement is not to substitute for a subscription or purchase of a work.

Endnotes

1. Copyright here means: "sole right and liberty of printing, reprinting, publishing and vending such map, chart, book or books, for the . . . term of fourteen years from the time of recording the title thereof in the clerk's office. . . ." Chapter XV, 1 Stat. 124 (May 31, 1790).
2. The act was entitled: "An act to amend the several acts respecting copy rights."
3. Copyright under this act became: "sole right and liberty of printing, reprinting, publishing, and vending such book or books, map, chart, musical composition, print, cut, or engraving, in whole or in part, for the term of twenty-eight years from the time of recording the title thereof, in the manner hereinafter directed." Chapter XVI, 4 Stat. 436 (February 3, 1831).
4. Section 5.
5. Under this act a copyright was: ". . . the sole liberty of printing, reprinting, publishing, completing, copying, executing, finishing, and vending the same [i.e., any book, map, chart, dramatic, or musical composition, engraving, cut, print or photograph or negative thereof, of a painting, drawing, chromo, statue, statuary, and of models or designs intended to be perfected as works of fine arts]; and in the case of a dramatic composition, of publicly performing or representing it, or causing it to be performed or representing by others; and authors may reserve the right to dramatize or translate their own works." Section 86.
6. Under section 97, the copyright notice is to read: "Entered according to act of Congress, in the year _____, by A.B., in the office of the librarian of Congress, at Washington."
7. Chapter 320 §§ 1, 64, 35 Stat.1075, 1088 (March 4, 1909).
8. 17 U.S.C. § 117, Pub. L. No. 96-517 § 10(b), 94 Stat. 3028 (December 12, 1980).
9. "Record Rental Amendment of 1984," Pub. L. 98-450, 98 Stat. 1727 (October 4, 1984).
10. "Computer Software Rental Amendments Act of 1989," Pub. L. 101-650, 104 Stat. 5134, 5135 Title VIII, §§ 802, 803 (December 1, 1990).
11. P.L. 101-553. See House Report (Judiciary Committee) No. 101-282(I),

October 13, 1989 [To accompany H.R. 3045], p.1 for discussion of purpose.
12. Pub. L. 101-650, 104 Stat. 5128, 5133 (December 1, 1990).
13. 17 U.S.C. § 102(a).
14. 17 U.S.C. § 102(b).
15. 17 U.S.C. § 109.
16. 17 U.S.C. § 109(b)(1)(A).
17. *Stewart* v. *Abend*, 495 U.S. 207, 237 (1990).
18. *Williams & Wilkins Co.* v. *United States*, 487 F.2d 1345, *aff'd*, 420 U.S. 376 (1975).
19. *Encyclopaedia Britannica, et al.* v. *Crooks*, 447 F. Supp. 243, 250-251 (1978).
20. *Stewart* v. *Abend*, 495 U.S. 207, 238 (1990).

TABLE 1.   What Can Be Copyrighted

As the copyright law was amended, more and more items were added to the list of things that could be copyrighted.

1790   Books, maps, and charts protected.

1802   Designs, engravings, and etchings added.

1831   Musical compositions added.

1856   Right of performance of dramatic works added.

1865   Photographs and negatives added.

1870   Paintings, statues, and other fine arts added; right to translate or dramatize granted to author.

1909   Rights of performance amended to include jukeboxes.

1912   Motion pictures added.

1952   Public performances for profit and recording of nondramatic literary works added to author's rights.

1976   copyright law amended to cover original works of authorship fixed in any tangible medium of expression, now known or later developed, from which they can be perceived, reproduced, or otherwise communicated, either directly or with the aid of a machine or device. Exceptions include works of industrial design and typefaces.

TABLE 2.   Duration of Copyright

As the copyright law was amended, the number of years that copyright protection was available increased. After expiration of a copyright, a work enters the public domain and can be freely copied.

1790   14 years with renewal for 14 years more.

1831   28 years with 14-year renewal.

1909   28 years with 28-year renewal (total 56 years).

1976   Life of the author plus 50 years.

For joint works, life of the surviving author plus 50 years.

For anonymous works, pseudonymous works, and works for hire: 75 years from year of first publication, or a term of 100 years from year of work's creation, whichever expires first.

Table 3.   Copyright Procedures

As the copyright law was amended, procedures for obtaining a copyright became less restrictive and more informal.

1790   Deposit required before publication in clerk's office of U.S. District Court.

Notice published in newspaper four times within two months of publication.

Copy deposited with Secretary of State within six months after publication.

No protection to imported works not written by a U.S. citizen.

Penalty: forfeiture.

Fines: 50 cents for each sheet found.

1802   Copyright notice required on or next to title page.

1831   Copyright notice required in each copy of work.

Newspaper notice no longer required except for renewals.

Deposit with District Clerk (transmittal to Secretary of State) required within 3 months of publication.

1834   Record of transfer or assignment of copyright required in the court of original entry.

1846   Delivery of copies to Smithsonian Institute and Library of Congress required.

1859   Repeal of 1846 deposit requirements.

Interior Department made copyright custodian.

1865   Deposit with Library of Congress required within one month of publication.

1867 $25 penalty for failure to deposit.

1870   Prepublication notice required.

Deposit of two copies within 10 days of publication to Library of Congress required.

Print titles must be filed before publication.

1874   Short form of copyright notice ("Copyright, 18__ , by A.B.") made legal.

Copyright extended to citizens of other nations if native country reciprocated and if copyrighted item was manufactured in the U.S.

1893   Copies deposited "on or before publication" have the same legal effect.

1895   No U.S. government publications are not copyrighted.

Penalties set for infringement of photographs and original works of art.

1897   Unauthorized, willful, and for-profit representation of any dramatic or musical composition becomes a misdemeanor punishable by imprisonment.

Appointment of a Register of Copyrights in Library of Congress.

Penalty set for printing false claim of copyright.

Importation of articles bearing false claim of copyright prohibited.

1900   U.S. copyright law extended to Hawaii.

1909   Copyright is effective by publication with statutory notice of copyright and deposit of two copies to the Library of Congress.

Manufacturing clause extended to include typesetting, printing, and binding within the U.S.

First sale doctrine established.

1955   U.S. recognized Universal Copyright Convention.

1956   Photographs of large, cumbersome works accepted in lieu of actual deposit.

1976   Omission of Copyright Notice does not result in immediate forfeiture.

Single national system established for both published and unpublished works.

Manufacturing clause terminated.

1988   Protection available to works distributed without copyright notice.

Deposit and registration requirement still necessary for infringement suit.

TABLE 4.   What is a Copyright?

The answer to this question depended on when it was asked.

1790   "sole right and liberty of printing, reprinting, publishing and vending such map, chart, book or books, for the . . . term of fourteen years
from the time of recording the title thereof in the clerk's office . . . ."
Chapter XV, 1 Stat. 124 (May 31, 1790).

1831   "sole right and liberty of printing, reprinting, publishing, and vending such book or books, map, chart, musical composition, print, cut,
or engraving, in whole or in part, for the term of twenty-eight years
from the time of recording the title thereof, in the manner hereinafter directed." Chapter XVI, 4 Stat. 436 (February 3, 1831).

1870   " . . . the sole liberty of printing, reprinting, publishing, completing,
copying, executing, finishing, and vending the same [i.e., any book,
map, chart, dramatic, or musical composition, engraving, cut, print
or photograph or negative thereof, of a painting, drawing, chromo,
statue, statuary, and of models or designs intended to be perfected
as works of fine arts]; and in the case of a dramatic composition, of
publicly performing or representing it, or causing it to be performed
or represented by others; and authors may reserve the right to
dramatize or translate their own works." 16 Stat.198 § 86 (July 8,
1870).

"That copyright shall be granted for the term of twenty-eight years
from the time of recording the title, thereof, in the manner hereinafter directed." § 87.

1909   " . . . the exclusive right:

a. To print, reprint, publish, copy, and vend the copyrighted work;

b. To translate the copyrighted work into other languages or dia-
lects, or make any other version thereof, if it be a literary work; to
dramatize it if it be a nondramatic work; to convert it into a novel or
other nondramatic work if it be a drama; to arrange or adapt it if it be
a musical work; to complete, execute, and finish it if it be a model or
design for a work of art;

c. To deliver, authorize the delivery of, read, or present the copyrighted work in public for profit if it be a lecture, sermon, address or
similar production, or other nondramatic literary work; to make or
procure the making of any transcription or record thereof by or from
which, in whole or in part, it may in any manner or by any method be
exhibited, delivered, presented, produced, or reproduced; and to
play or perform it in public for profit, and to exhibit, represent,
produce, or reproduce it in any manner or by any method
whatsoever. . .

d. To perform or represent the copyrighted work publicly if it be a drama or, if it be a dramatic work and not reproduced in copies for sale, to vend any manuscript or any record whatsoever thereof; to make or to procure the making of any transcription or record thereof by or from which, in whole or in part, it may in any manner or by any method be exhibited, performed, represented, produced, or reproduced; and to exhibit, perform, represent, produce, or reproduce it in any manner or by any method whatsoever; and

e. To perform the copyrighted work publicly for profit if it be a musical composition; and for the purpose of public performance for profit, and for the purposes set forth in subsection (a) hereof, to make any arrangement or setting of it or of the melody of it in any system of notation or any form or record in which the thought of an author may be recorded and from which it may be read or reproduced . . . ."

1978   "Copyright protection subsists . . . in original works of authorship fixed in any tangible medium of expression, now known or later developed, from which they can be perceived, reproduced, or otherwise communicated, either directly or with the aid of a machine or device.

Copyright in a work created on or after January 1, 1978, subsists from its creation and . . . endures for a term consisting of the life of the author and fifty years after the author's death."

4

International Copyright Law

- *Is there an international copyright law that will protect an author's right in every country?*

- *Do librarians have to consult the copyright laws of other countries before photocopying works copyrighted outside the United States?*

- *How do the international copyright agreements that the United States has signed with other countries affect American libraries?*

HISTORY

Copyright law in England formed the basis of copyright law in the United States until the American Revolution. After independence from Britain, however, the U.S. copyright law went its own way. In fact, U. S. copyright law followed a different path from that of most other major nations of the world until very recently.

Unlike England, the United States was slow to offer copyright protection for many types of creative works. The first U.S. copyright statute in 1790 covered only books, maps, and charts. In 1802, the U.S. law was extended to include engravings—an addition that had been made in England 68 years earlier.

Authors were also relieved of many of the formalities for obtaining a copyright in other countries long before such changes were made in the United States. Up until 1978, if a work was published in the United States without a copyright notice, the copyright was irretrievably lost. The requirement that copies be deposited was dropped in many countries. Today, authors are still required to deposit copies of their works before bringing an infringement suit.

The period for which a copyright is effective has also been extended rather slowly in the United States. The English copyright law of 1842 made the period of coverage the life of the author plus seven years. Up until 1978, the U.S. copyright extended only to a maximum of 56 years.

The United States was also slow to involve itself in international copyright protection. In England, the International Copyright Act of 1886 enabled Great Britain to sign an international agreement, the Berne Convention for the Protection of Literary and Artistic Works (better known as the Berne Convention). The United States did not pass an act allowing it to sign the same international agreement until 1988—102 years later.

LEGAL CONCEPTS

There are two important things that every librarian should understand about international copyright law.

First, there is no such thing as an international copyright law that automatically protects an author's creative works in every nation of the world. To protect their works worldwide, authors would have to comply with the copyright law of each individual nation—an impossible task.[1] In order to protect their works in as many nations as possible, authors instead must rely on the existing international copyright agreements between many countries.

Second, the copyrights of other countries generally do not have any effect in the United States unless the United States has signed a copyright convention or treaty with that country.[2] Signatories of copyright conventions or treaties generally receive the same copyright protection that member countries provide to their own citizens.

This means that libraries have two options when it comes to copying, performing, or publicly displaying works that are copyrighted in a foreign country but not in the United States:

1. They can try to determine if the work is protected under the U.S. copyright law by an international copyright treaty, or other agreement.

2. They can treat every foreign work as if it had a valid U.S. copyright.

INTERNATIONAL COPYRIGHT CONVENTIONS

Why would the United States be interested in international copyright protection? The United States is the world's largest exporter of copyrighted material—especially books, sound recordings, motion pictures, and computer software. Copyrighted materials routinely generate a trade surplus for the United States, but piracy cuts deeply in countries that are the biggest market for U.S. creative works. The only effective solution to this problem is membership in an international copyright treaty or conference.

There are two major international copyright conventions in the world today. The United States is now a member of both—the Universal Copyright Convention of 1952 (UCC) and the Berne Convention. Both of these agreements require members to accord to the nationals of other member countries the same level of copyright protection that they provide to their own citizens. Both are administered by United Nations agencies: UCC is administered by the United Nations Educational, Scientific, and Cultural Organization (UNESCO) and the Berne Convention is administered by the World Intellectual Property Organization (WIPO).

There is, however, a significant difference between the two conventions. UCC is a *unilateral* agreement. There are no requirements that member countries adhere to certain standards to be members. A member nation of UCC may provide little protection of its own citizens' rights, but it is not required to raise those standards in order to become a member. That nation would probably provide little protection to fellow members as well, since it is only obligated to protect to the level it provides to its own citizens. The Berne Convention is, however, a *bilateral* agreement. Each individual country must adhere to a certain minimal level of copyright protection for its own citizens before being allowed to sign. This guarantees that each member country is assured of certain basic protections.

UCC: The United States was a founding member of the UCC, which went into force in the United States on September 16, 1955. The UCC was created largely to give United States works some form of international copyright protection. In general, works copyrighted in any UCC countries are treated in the U.S. as if they had completed all the procedures required by the U.S. copyright law. More than 80 countries are members of UCC.

Berne Convention: The Berne Convention of 1886 is the oldest international copyright agreement. It is also the major multilateral agreement governing international copyright in the world today. The U.S. joined the Berne Convention for several reasons:[3]

- *Protection.* It would secure the highest available level of multilateral copyright protection. UCC offered only minimum protection that did not deter piracy. It was estimated that U.S. companies lost between $43 billion and $61 billion during 1986 because of inadequate protection for U.S. intellectual property.
- *Additional Rights.* In addition to the general rights available under UCC, members of the Berne Convention are guaranteed protection under the laws of other states: duration of copyright for life of the author plus 50 years; rights of translation, reproduction, public performance, broadcasting, adaptation, and arrangement.
- *More Countries.* The United States immediately gained copyright relations with 24 countries with which it previously had no current relations.
- *International Policy.* U.S. membership in the Berne Convention also makes it possible for the United States to participate in the formulation and management of international copyright policy.

In short, membership in the Berne Convention was clearly in the national interest because it ensures a "strong, credible U.S. presence in the global marketplace."[4] In exchange for these benefits, member nations receive copyright protection in the United States at the same level as works published in the U.S.

CHANGES NEEDED IN U.S. LAW

The Berne Convention did not take effect in the United States until March 1, 1989. This was largely because of major obstacles in the U.S. law itself—the manufacturing clause, the copyright notice requirement, the deposit requirement, the registration requirement, and the duration of copyright protection. The United States amended its copyright statute only where there were clear conflicts and only to the extent necessary to comply with the requirements of the Berne Convention.

Manufacturing clause: When it became part of the United States copyright law in 1891 as a compromise, the manufacturing clause was an attempt to induce printing of an edition of a work in the United States to help bolster the U.S. printing industry. Despite numerous amendments that added many exceptions and qualifications, books and periodicals in the English language were required to be manufactured in the United States to receive full copyright protection right up until 1981.

The difficulties in completely eliminating this requirement for the U.S. printing industry were very evident in the concerns it raised when a new copyright law was being debated in 1976. The legislative committee stated that "there is no justification on principle for a manufacturing requirement in the copyright statute, and although there may have been some economic justification for it at one time, that justification no longer exists." Despite this, the repeal was postponed and did not actually occur until July 1, 1986.

Copyright Notice: A substantial roadblock to signing the Berne Convention was the U.S. requirement that each copy of a work bear a notice of copyright. This mandatory notice was considered inconsistent with the Berne Convention prohibition on formalities.

The notice had served to alert users that copyright was claimed and may have prevented many instances of unintentional infringement. It also made it easy to determine the first year of publication. Librarians also found the notice on the verso of the title page a useful means of determining who owned the copyright to ask for permission to copy.

A compromise was struck. The notice was no longer required to be placed on all publicly distributed copies in order to obtain a copyright, but an incentive was added. If the notice is present and the work is infringed, the courts will not allow a defendant to claim "innocent infringement"—that is, to claim that they did not realize that the work was protected—and thus receive a reduction in the damages awarded to the copyright owner.

Deposit: Another roadblock was the deposit requirement. Like the notice requirement, it was a prohibited formality under the Berne Convention. A compromise also was struck here. Deposit is mandatory for all works published in the United States under copyright protection. The owner of a copyright has a legal obligation to deposit a copy of the finished work with the Library of Congress within a specified time or be fined or subject to other penalties. Failure to deposit, however, does not affect copyright protection.

Registration: A further roadblock and prohibitive formality under the Berne Convention was the registration requirement. Under the current law, registration is not generally a requirement for obtaining a copyright. Before an infringement suit can be filed in court, however, registration is necessary for works published in the United States or for works from non-Berne Convention countries. If registration is not made within three months of publication only an award of actual damages and profits is available. Statutory damages and attorney's fees are lost.

Duration of Copyright: Up until 1978, the period of time that copyright protection was available to an author or copyright owner was a total of 56 years. After that period of time, the work was in the public domain. In contrast, the large majority of the world's countries had adopted a term of life of the author plus fifty years. The arguments made for bringing the U.S. term in line with the rest of the world were:

1. The existing term was not long enough to ensure authors and their families a fair economic return on their labors. Life expectancy has increased substantially since the terms were set in 1909.
2. The commercial life of creative works had been substantially lengthened because of technological advances.
3. Authors were harmed and the public received no real benefit from such a short term. Works in the public domain often cost no less than those still under copyright. Also, publishers were reluctant to invest in works to which they had no exclusive publishing rights.
4. The death of an author is a definite and fixed date, making the duration of copyright easier to calculate. Also, all of an author's works would fall into the public domain at the same time.
5. The previous system of coyright renewal was confusing and often resulted in an inadvertent and unjust loss of copyright.
6. The new system would be fairer to authors who have lost the perpetual rights to their works with the end of the state common law.
7. The rest of the world recognized a longer period of protection than the United States. This created a disparity, causing some nations to threaten retaliation and resulting in unnecessary complications in international business dealings.[5]

A registry of death dates and a system of presumptions was established as the result of this act.

Moral Rights

The most extensive debate in Congress concerning the United States joining the Berne Convention centered on the non-economic rights of authors in the Berne Convention. These moral rights are known as rights of paternity and integrity.

Paternity is the right of authors to claim authorship of their works. Integrity is the right of authors to object to distortion, mutilation, or other alteration of a work, or derogatory action that would damage their honor or reputation in relation to their work.[6] Congress concluded that existing U.S. law—including the current copyright law, the Lanham Act, various state statutes, and common law principles developed by U.S. courts such as libel, defamation, misrepresentation, and unfair competition—provides sufficient protection to allow the United States to meet these requirements of the Berne Convention.

Overall, however, the Berne Convention itself is not enforceable in U.S. courts. It is not self-executing. As with the UCC, neither the fact that the United States adheres to Berne nor the provisions of the convention itself can form the basis for a claim in the United States that does not already exist in U.S. copyright law. The effect of the United States' adherence to an international copyright convention is thus limited to the changes made to U.S. law. The convention itself adds no additional rights.

DETERMINING A COURSE OF ACTION

There are two ways to deal with foreign works that are not copyrighted in the United States.

1. Determine if the work is protected under the United States copyright law.
2. Treat the work as if it is protected under U.S. copyright law.

To determine if a foreign work is covered involves some investigation. First, it is necessary to determine if the foreign country is a member of one of the international copyright conventions to which the United States is a signatory. It must also be determined when that country became a signatory. The Berne Convention and the UCC are not retroactive.

The second method means treating every work as if it were copyrighted. This is the safest approach and may be the easiest course to take.

Endnotes

1. Many nations require copyright owners to be either nationals or legal residents of their country. Also, several nations offer no real protection to an author.
2. Exceptions to this are unpublished works which are covered no matter what the nationality or domicile of the author. So are works first pub-

lished by the U.N. or O.A.S. and works that come within the scope of a Presidential Proclamation. See 17 U.S.C.§104.

3. These reasons are set forth in Senate Report (Judiciary Committee) No. 100-352, May 20, 1988 [To accompany S.1301], pp. 2-4.

4. Senate Report (Judiciary Committee) No. 100-352, May 20, 1988[To accompany S. 1301], p.2.

5. These arguments are set forth on pages 134-135 of House Report (Judiciary Committee) No. 94-1476, September 3, 1976 [To accompany S. 22].

6. Article 6bis of the Berne Convention.

PART II

Library Applications

5
Printed Materials

- *When someone buys a book, what rights does he or she have or not have?*

- *If I want to copy something from a book, should I ask the author for permission?*

- *Is it okay for my library to buy certain magazines and another library to buy other magazines, then for us to swap copies of articles?*

WORD OF CAUTION

The next four chapters provide general information on copyright law. Of course, whenever a specific problems arises, it is always best to seek legal counsel but most libraries have little or no budget for this kind of expense. For this reason, the next best practice is to become familiar with the copyright law, to be diligent in keeping current on changes, and to err on the side of caution. We call this practice *defensive law*.

Copyright law is constantly changing. Professional journals often contain news about important developments in copyright. Keeping a file with copies of such articles, as long as they are from a variety of journals published at different times, seems to be well within "fair use" guidelines and can serve as a reference resource when questions arise.

BASIC PRINCIPLES

Understanding the purpose behind the federal copyright law is an important first step toward understanding the law itself. The founding fathers were concerned with protecting the rights of authors and inventors and encouraging creative thinking, but they also knew that the ideas and inventions of creative people were valuable to the populace as a whole, which needs access to ideas and inventions to be productive citizens able to function in a free society.

The first copyright laws, passed in 1783 by all of the colonies except Delaware, protected *only* printed matter. Every copyright law passed in the United States since that early law has included protection of printed matter, as well as an ever increasing range of other formats.

What kind of protection does the copyright law of today afford printed materials? Consider this example. Imagine a person going into a bookstore and purchasing a newly published, copyrighted book. He or she has purchased the physical object called the book and may do many things with that book. The book owner may keep the book, sell it, lend it, write in it, color it, throw it away, burn it or tear out pages. The person who owns a particular copy of a book may freely do with it as he or she please—to a point.

The purchaser of a book *does not* own the copyright to that book and therefore cannot copy it. The author or publisher has the copyright and does not forfeit it when a copy of the book is sold. To illustrate this idea lets look again at a specific situation. What if the book purchaser says, "Since I have had this book signed by the author, I want to preserve it in pristine condition. So, I'm going to copy a chapter a week on my copy machine at work, and when I've completed the copying, I'll put the copy in a three-ring notebook on my desk for reference. That way, I'll have the use of the contents while maintaining the value of the original." Well, that would be a clear copyright violation. The purchaser of the book did not obtain the right to make copies of the book—all he or she got was *one* copy (the one that was purchased).[1]

It is important to interject a piece of information here that may seem obvious but that many people overlook: *one can always seek the permission of the author or publisher to copy a work. If such permission is granted, with or without a fee, in writing, then go ahead and copy.* In dealing with journals and other serials, it is usually possible to work out a fee schedule through the Copyright Clearance Center[2] for the copying of articles. In either of these cases—written permission or payment of fees—the spirit of the copyright law is fully upheld.

But what if there's no time to get permission? What if all that's needed is an occasional journal article? What privileges and restrictions apply to library books and other printed materials? Well, for everyone, including the purchaser of the book mentioned above, there are some exceptions to the "no copying without permission or payment" edict. Limited copying of copyrighted, printed materials may be done under the doctrine of fair use.

The notion of fair use was created by the courts. No copyright law until the latest actually incorporated this idea. Until 1976, it was only in the case law (decisions by the courts) that the concept of fair use appeared, not in the statutes themselves. Now, it is codified into law in Section 107 of 17 U.S.C. (the Copyright Act of 1976).

Fair use allows the copying, in particular circumstances, of parts of a copyrighted work without permission of the copyright owner. Fair use may best be described by a quote from the case *Rosemont Enters* v. *Random House, Inc.*, 366 F. 2d 303, 306 (2d Cir. 1966), which says that fair use is the "privilege in others than the owner to use the copyrighted material in a reasonable manner" without consent "notwithstanding the monopoly granted to the owner." In other words, the fair use doctrine tries to balance the rights of the copyright holder with the public's need for information.

Elements of Fair Use

Section 107 of 17 U.S.C. (the Copyright Act of 1976), entitled "The Limitations on Exclusive Rights: Fair Use," states that:

> . . . the fair use of a copyrighted work . . . for purposes such as criticism, comment, news reporting, teaching (including multiple copies for classroom use), scholarship, or research, is not an infringement of copyright.

In determining whether the use made of a work in any particular case is a fair use, the factors to be considered include:

1. The purpose and character of the use, including whether such use is of a commercial nature or is for nonprofit educational purposes.
2. The nature of the copyrighted work.
3. The amount and substantiality of the portion used in relation to the copyrighted work as a whole.
4. The effect of the use upon the potential market for or value of the copyrighted work.

These factors have not been defined in the law, so it is necessary to study court cases to determine what the words "purpose and character of the use," "the nature of the copyrighted work," and "amount and substantiality of the portion used" mean. In an 1841 case,[3] it was stated:

> . . . it is certainly not necessary, to constitute an invasion of copyright, that the whole of a work should be copied, or even a larger portion of it, in form or in substance. If so much is taken that the value of the original is sensibly diminished, or the labors of the original author are substantially to an injurious extent appropriated by another, that is sufficient, in point of law, to constitute a privacy pro tanta. . . . Neither does it necessarily depend upon the quantity taken, whether it is an infringement of the copyright or not. It is often affected by other considerations, the value of the materials taken, and the importance of it to the sale of the original work.

Copy Machines and Libraries

So what does all of this mean for those of you who work in libraries and have patrons coming in every day wanting to copy the materials held by your institution? *The safest course for a library to follow is to have an unsupervised, coin-operated copy machine available for the use of patrons.*

This copy machine should have a notice of copyright on or near it. This copyright notice should state:

> NOTICE: The Copyright Law of the United States (Title 17 United States Code) governs the making of photocopies of copyrighted material. The person using this equipment is liable for any infringement.[4]

Patrons, whether they are students or the general public, are thereby notified that it is their responsibility to stay within the parameters of fair use. This doesn't mean that library staff can't give patrons technical advice about how to use the copier. It does mean, however, that it is best left to the patron to decide what constitutes fair use in each situation.

This policy of letting the patron assume responsibility for copying what is needed carries over into other areas of library service as well. For example, imagine that there is a poetry discussion group meeting in your library. In the name of efficiency, you might think about making a dozen copies of a poem that will be used in the discussions— one for each person who has signed up so far. Don't do it. If you must make the copies yourself, obtain written permission from the publisher or the author, and then make the permitted number of copies. If time constraints make this impossible, purchase additional copies of the work or locate an edition in the public domain (if that is possible).

It is very important to get any permissions in writing. In one instance recently, a library network organization planned a poetry discussion series. The series was to be held in a number of the network's libraries at the same time. Because of this, it was decided that an anthology of the selected poems would be printed in a quantity that would allow each participant to have one. Seven publishers were contacted by telephone, and all gave verbal permission for the requested copying. Letters confirming the permissions were received within a week from six of the publishing houses contacted. With this assurance, the materials were sent off to be copied. About a week later, at the same time that the finished poetry anthologies arrived at the library network headquarters, a letter arrived from that seventh publisher. Everyone assumed that a written permission for use of the requested material was contained therein. No such luck. The letter stated that the network was not to use the poem from that publisher's work and that the person who had given permission on the phone was not authorized to do so. The network staff spent the afternoon razoring that particular poem out of the anthology.

Happily, it is seldom that permission is withheld by a publisher (or author) if the request is reasonable. Both publishers and authors see value in allowing the use of a sample of their work. Sometimes there will be a fee. Fees vary widely and are entirely negotiable, so don't give up if you are told that a fee is expected. Publishers and authors recognize that most libraries are not rich institutions, and they are often willing to reduce or forgo their standard fees.

Fair Use Guidelines for Classroom Copying

Section 107 of the present copyright law has a number of provisions that are important for teachers, as well as librarians. School library media specialists should be familiar with the rules regarding copying by teachers, since the teacher may make a request that the media specialist do the copying or see that it is done.

Because fair use is a somewhat vague concept, concerned groups were eager to have guidelines that were more clearly defined than the law itself. Representatives from the Ad Hoc Committee of Educational Institutions and Organizations on Copyright Revision, the Authors League of America, Inc., and the Association of American Publishers, Inc., came together and agreed upon guidelines that have been given heavy weight in the courts. These guidelines are for classroom copying in not-for-profit educational institutions and apply to the copying of both books and periodicals. It is important to note that the guidelines state the minimum and not the maximum standards of educational fair use and that the conditions determining the extent of permissible copying for educational purposes may change in the future. Uses that are permissible now may not be permissible in the future and vice-versa. Those guidelines are as follow:

Teachers may make a single copy for themselves, for research or for teaching purposes of:

- a chapter in a book
- an article from a periodical or newspaper
- a short story, short essay, or short poem, whether or not it is from a collective work
- a chart, graph, diagram, drawing, cartoon, or picture from a book, periodical, or newspaper.

These privileges are subject to the following restrictions:

1. Copies may not be used for anthologies, compilations, or collective works.
2. Consumable materials, such as *workbooks, exercises, standardized tests, and answer sheets may not be copied.*
3. Copying may not be used to substitute for purchasing.
4. Copying, as a substitute for purchasing, cannot be "directed by higher authority."
5. Copying cannot be repeated "with respect to the same item by the same teacher from term to term."
6. The student may not be charged, if there is a charge, more than the actual costs of photocopying.

Teachers also have certain privileges in regard to making copies for their students. Teachers can make multiple copies (one copy for each pupil, that is) for classroom use if the copying meets three tests, *but only if the copies carry a notice of copyright.* The three tests are brevity, spontaneity, and cumulative effect.

Brevity. The first test is for brevity. Brevity has been defined in the guidelines as:

- a complete poem if less than 250 words and if printed on not more than two pages or an excerpt from a poem of not more than 250 words
- a complete article, story, or essay of less than 2,500 words or an excerpt of not more than 1,000 words or 10 percent of a work, whichever is less, but in any event a *minimum* of 500 words
- one chart, graph, diagram, drawing, cartoon, or picture per book or per periodical issue.

For "special" works, i.e., when certain works in poetry, prose, or in "poetic prose," which often combine language with illustrations and are intended sometimes for children and at other times for a more general audience, fall short of 2,500 words in their entirety, the limit is an excerpt of not more than two published pages and not more than 10 percent of the words found in the text. These "special" works may *not* be reproduced in their entirety.

Spontaneity. The second test is for spontaneity, which is defined in this way:

1. The copying must be at the instance and inspiration of the individual teacher.
2. The inspiration and decision to use the work and the maximum teaching effectiveness must be so close in time that it would be unreasonable to expect a timely reply to a request for permission.

Cumulative Effect. The final test is for cumulative effect which means:

1. The copying must be for only one course in the school.
2. Not more than one short poem, article, story, essay or two excerpts may be copied from the same author, nor more than three from the same collective work or periodical volume during one class term.
3. Multiple copying is limited to no more than nine instances for one course during one class term.

These limitations do not apply to current news periodicals and newspapers and current news sections of other periodicals.
The full text of these guidelines appears at the end of this chapter.

Copying Privileges for Libraries and Archives

In addition to the privileges accorded under fair use, there is another section of the copyright law, Section 108, that extends special privileges to qualifying libraries and archives. Entitled "Reproduction by Libraries and Archives," Section 108 allows libraries or archives that meet certain criteria to make and/or distribute copies of printed materials. This right to copy and distribute does not apply, with minor exceptions, to:

· musical, pictorial, graphic, or sculptural works,

- motion pictures or other audiovisual works, except audiovisual works dealing with the news.

Section 108. It is not an infringement of copyright for a library or archives, or any of its employees acting within the scope of their employment, to reproduce one copy of a work, or to distribute such a copy, if the following conditions are met:

1. The reproduction or distribution is made without any purpose of direct or indirect commercial advantage.
2. The collections of the library or archives are open to the public or are available not only to researchers affiliated with the library or archives or with the institution of which it is a part, but also to other persons doing research in a specialized field.[5]
3. The reproduction or distribution of the work includes a notice of copyright.[6]

Once these conditions have been met, libraries and archives can make a copy of the following:

1. An entire unpublished work, but only for purposes of preservation and security or for research use in another library or archive. The receiving institution must meet certain criteria, and the unpublished material must be part of the current collection of the first library or archives.[7]
2. An entire published work, but only for the purpose of replacement of a copy that is damaged, deteriorating, lost, or stolen, if the library or archives has, after a reasonable effort, determined that an unused replacement can't be obtained at a fair price.[8]
3. An entire copyrighted work, or a substantial part of an out-of-print work, if a user requests such material and the library or archive where the request is made has first determined, on the basis of a reasonable investigation, that a copy of the work cannot be obtained at a fair price.[9] Under these circumstances if a library or archive does not have the requested work, it may also request that another institution copy it. These conditions apply in cases where:
   - the copy becomes the property of the user
   - the library or archive has had no notice that the copy will be used for any purpose other than private study, scholarship or research
   - the library or archives displays prominently, at the place where orders are accepted and on its order forms, a warning of copyright in accordance with the regulations developed by the Register of Copyrights.[10]

Furthermore, a library or archives may copy portions of a written

work for a requesting library or archives user, whose request may be
for material from the library or archives where the request is made or
may be for material from another library or archives, if:

1. No more than one article or other contribution to a copyrighted
   collection or periodical issue.

*(Note that the "Rule of Five" applies to the copying of periodical
articles. That is: For a periodical title published within the previous
five years, a requesting library may make no more than five requests
for copies of articles—whether for the same article for different
patrons or for different articles for the same or different patrons—
from the same title, whether from one or more than one library. Once
this limit has been met, there is a presumption that the requesting
library needs to buy a subscription to the periodical. Alternatively, the
library may pay copying fees to the Copyright Clearance Center. The
responsibility for keeping records of interlibrary loan transactions
rests with the requesting library.)*

2. A small part of any other copyrighted work, if:
   • the copy becomes the property of the user
   • the library or archives has had no notice that the copy will be used
     for any purpose other than private study, scholarship, or research,
     and
   • the library or archives displays prominently, at the place where
     orders are taken and on its order forms, a warning of copyright in
     accordance with regulations prescribed by the Register of
     Copyrights.[11]
3. A substantial part of a copyrighted work when, after a reasonable
   investigation,[12] the library or archives where the request originates
   determines that the work cannot be obtained at a fair price, if:
   • the copy becomes the property of the user
   • the library or archives has had no notice that the copy will be used
     for any purpose other than private study, scholarship, or research,
     and
   • the library or archives displays prominently, at the place where
     orders are taken and on its order forms, a warning of copyright in
     accordance with the regulations developed by the Register of
     Copyrights.[13]

"Isolated and Unrelated." The rights of reproduction and distribution under Section 108 pertain to the "isolated" and "unrelated"
reproduction or distribution of a single copy of the same material on
separate occasions. They do not extend to cases where library employees are aware of or have substantial reason to believe that someone is
engaging in the reproduction of multiple copies of the same material.

It is important to remember that the privileges of both Sections 107 and 108 are always available. One section does not cancel the other.

Networks

Libraries cooperate in order to stretch their budgets to the maximum. While cooperative projects are, on the whole, to be admired, there are some cautions that must be given, While the copyright law does not absolutely stop a library from any legitimate activity, in the spirit of cooperation, it is easy to make plans that seem very practical but which could be in violation of the copyright law.

Here's an example. Three academic libraries form a consortium with the specific purpose of saving money on the purchase of journals, which we all know are expensive and getting more so. While all of the libraries buy certain titles that are used frequently on site, there are nine rather esoteric ones that none of the three libraries uses on a regular basis. These journals are titled A, B, C, D, E, F, G, H, and I. The first academic library volunteers to buy A, B and C. The second library agrees to purchase D, E, and F. And the third library takes the remaining three. The libraries initially agree they will each provide copies of articles requested by the other libraries from the particular journals that they alone are purchasing as part of the cooperative agreement. Can these libraries do that?

The answer is no. As stated in section 108 (g)(2) of the copyright law:

> . . . nothing in this clause prevents a library or archives from participating in interlibrary arrangements that do not have, as their *purpose or effect*, that the library or archives receiving such copies or phonorecords for distribution does so in such aggregate quantities as to substitute for a *subscription* to or purchase of such work. [emphasis added].

However, these libraries may loan the whole periodical each time a request is made for an article, as many times as necessary to fulfill requests. In addition to the rights given under the act, there is always the possibility of:

- using material in the public domain which is no longer protected by the copyright law.
- requesting permission of the copyright owner.
- purchasing additional copies of the work.
- acquiring a copy from an authorized agent who will fulfill any copyright requirements to get the copy.
- paying a fee to the owner of the copyright or to a copyright clearance center.

Five-Year Review

The privileges given to teachers, libraries and archives, and their patrons are considerable. Publishers often express dismay at the allowances made for copying under the existing copyright law, and one can readily see why there is reservation on the part of those whose livelihood depends on the sale of copyrighted materials. It is of extreme importance that those to whom the privileges extend take care to stay within the limits of the law. As a check on uncontrolled copying, Section 108 includes the following clause:

> Five years from the effective date of this Act, and at five-year intervals thereafter, the Register of Copyrights, after consulting with representatives of authors, book and periodical publishers, and other owners of copyrighted materials, and with representatives of library users and librarians, shall submit to the Congress a report setting forth the extent to which this section has achieved the intended statutory balancing of the rights of creators, and the needs of users. The report should also describe any problems that may have arisen, and present legislative or other recommendations, if warranted.

Put in simple terms, this means, "Abuse it and lose it." That's why it is essential that the staffs of all types of libraries become familiar with and keep current with the provisions of United States copyright law.

CASE STUDY

You are the reference librarian for a library in Iowa that has a wonderful local history collection. People doing research on their family histories often come in and use the materials.

In today's mail you have received a request from a gentleman residing in California. It seems that his family lived for many years in your town in Iowa and that much of the family's history is contained in a book in your local history room entitled "The Smythes of Durwin, Iowa." This book does not circulate, so the man has requested that you copy the book for him at his expense.

Because of budget cuts, library staffing is at a minimum, so the man's request is somewhat annoying to you. On the other hand, you can appreciate his interest in seeing the material, especially since he seems to be sure that what he's looking for is contained in the volume the library holds. His offer to pay whatever price you set is further proof of his interest and need.

One of the high schoolers who works as a page in the library agrees to copy the work, admittedly for the extra money. After she has begun the job, your library director happens to stop by and asks about the copying going on. You describe the project. The director asks, "What about copyright?"

You have to admit that you hadn't thought about the issue. What is your answer to the director?   *Answer.* Your first task is to determine whether or not the book is in the public domain. If it is, there's no copyright problem. To make that determination, look to the history chapter of this book as a starting point. Using the publication date and the tables for the appropriate version of the copyright law, you may be able to ascertain whether or not the copyright is still in effect. If you don't feel able to make this determination yourself, the Library of Congress has a service which, for a fee, will help with such questions.

If the book is under copyright, there are several steps you can take. First, you can seek the permission of the copyright holder to do the copying. Such permission may be free or may include a fee. If you cannot get written permission, due to time constraints or because you are unable to locate the copyright holder to obtain such permission, then a study of Sections 107 and 108 may help you determine whether or not to consult an attorney.

FULL TEXT: GUIDELINES

Agreement on Guidelines for Classroom Copying in Not-For-Profit Educational Institutions With Respect to Books and Periodicals

The purpose of the following guidelines is to state the minimum and not the maximum standards of educational fair use under Section 107 of H.R. 2223. The parties agree that the conditions determining the extent of permissible copying for educational purposes may change in the future; that certain types of copying permitted under these guidelines may not be permissible in the future; and conversely that in the future other types of copying not permitted under these guidelines may be permitted under revised guidelines.

Moreover, the following statement of guidelines is not intended to limit the types of copying permitted under the standards of fair use by judicial decision, which are stated in Section 107 of the Copyright Revision Bill. There may be instances in which copying that does not fall within the guidelines stated below may nonetheless be permitted under the criteria of fair use.

I. Single Copying for Teachers

A single copy may be made of any of the following by or for a teacher at his or her individual request for his or her scholarly research or use in teaching or preparation to teach a class:

A. A chapter from a book;

B. An article from a periodical or newspaper;

C. A short story, short essay or short poem, whether or not from a collective work;

D. A chart, graph, diagram, drawing, cartoon or picture from a book, periodical, or newspaper.

II. Multiple Copies for Classroom Use

Multiple copies (not to exceed in any event more than one copy per pupil in a course) may be made by or for the teacher giving the course for classroom use or discussion, *provided that*:

A. The copying meets the tests of brevity and spontaneity as defined below; and,

B. The copying meets the cumulative effect test as defined below; and,

C. Each copy includes a notice of copyright.

Definitions

Brevity

i.   *Poetry: a) A complete poem if less than 250 words and if printed on not more than two pages, or; b) from a longer poem, an excerpt of not more than 250 words.*

ii.   *Prose: a) Either a complete article, story or essay of less than 2,500 words, or; b) an excerpt from any prose work of not more than 1,000 words or 10% of the work, whichever is less, but in any event a minimum of 500 words.*

[Each of the numerical limits stated in "i" and "ii" above may be expanded to permit the completion of an unfinished prose paragraph.]

iii.*Illustration: One chart, graph, diagram, drawing, cartoon, or picture per book or per periodical issue.*

iv.   *"Special" works: Certain works in poetry, prose or in "poetic prose" which often combine language with illustrations and which are intended sometimes for children and at other times for a more general audience that fall short of 2,500 words in their entirety. Paragraph "ii" above notwithstanding such "special works" may not be reproduced in their entirety; however, an excerpt comprising not more than two of the published pages of such special work and containing not more than 10% of the words found in the text thereof, may be reproduced.*

Spontaneity

i.   The copying is at the instance and inspiration of the individual teacher; and,

ii.   The inspiration and decision to use the work and the moment of its use for maximum teaching effectiveness are so close in time that it would be unreasonable to expect a timely reply to a request for permission.

Cumulative Effect

i.   The copying of the material is for only one course in the school in which the copies are made.

ii.   Not more than one short poem, article, story, essay or two excerpts may be copied from the same author, nor more than three from the same collective work or periodical volume during one class term.

iii. There shall not be more than nine instances of such multiple copying for one course during one class term.

[The limitations stated in "ii" and "iii" above shall not apply to current news periodicals and newspapers and current news sections of other periodicals.]

III. Prohibitions as to I and II above

Notwithstanding any of the above the following shall be prohibited :

A. Copying shall not be used to create or to replace or substitute for anthologies, compilations or collective works. Such replacements or substitution may occur whether copies of various works or excerpts therefrom are accumulated or reproduced and used separately.

B. There shall be no copying of or from works intended to be "consumable" in the course of study or of teaching. These include workbooks, exercises, standardized texts and test booklets and answer sheets and like consumable material.

C. Copying shall not:

a. substitute for the purchase of books, publishers' reprints or periodicals;

b. be directed by higher authority;

c. be repeated with respect to the same item by the same teacher from term to term.

D. No charge shall be made to the student beyond the actual cost of the photocopying.

Endnotes

1. As stated in 17 U.S.C. 202: "Ownership of a copyright, or of any of the exclusive rights under a copyright, is distinct from ownership of any material object in which the work is embodied. Transfer of ownership of any material object, including the copy or phonorecord in which the work is first fixed, does not of itself convey any rights in the copyrighted work embodied in the object; nor, in the absence of an agreement, does transfer of ownership of a copyright or of any exclusive rights under a copyright convey property rights in any material object."

2. The Copyright Clearance Center, Inc., is located at 27 Congress Street, Salem, Massachusetts 01970. Their phone number is (508) 744-3350.

Their FAX number is (508) 741-2318. The Center currently registers more than 1.5 million titles.

3. *Folsom* v. *Marsh*, F. Cas. No. 4901, 2 Story 100 (1841, CC Mass). See also Chapter 3.

4. There is no type size required by law for the notice but it should be at least 18 points in size.

5. This would make libraries in for-profit organizations eligible for protection under this section provided they only engaged in isolated, spontaneous making of single photocopies and the library was available to persons doing research in the field who are not affiliated with the for-profit organization.

6. This notice could be made by a rubber stamp and state: "This work may be copyrighted."

7. Only unpublished works can be reproduced under this exemption but it extends to any type of work, including photographs, motion pictures, and sound recordings. House Report (Judiciary Committee) No.94-1476, Sept. 3, 1976 [To accompany S.22] states on page 75: "Under this exemption, for example, a repository could make photocopies of manuscripts by microfilm or electrostatic process, but could not reproduce the work in 'machine-readable' language for storage in an information system."

8. House Report (Judiciary Committee) No.94-1476, Sept. 3, 1976 [To accompany S.22], states that while this exemption is limited to unpublished works, it can be any type of unpublished work, including photographs, motion pictures, and sound recordings. It also states on page 75 that: "Under this exemption, for example, a repository could make photocopies of manuscripts by microfilm or electrostatic process, but could not reproduce the work in 'machine-readable' language for storage in an information system."

9. This search would have to include at least checking with the publisher and the well-known reprint agents. House Report (Judiciary Committee) No.94-1476, Sept. 3, 1976 [To accompany S.22], states on pages 75-76: "The scope and nature of a reasonable investigation to determine that an unused replacement cannot be obtained will vary according to the circumstances of a particular situation. It will always require recourse to commonly-known trade sources in the United States, and in the normal situation also to the publisher or other copyright owner (if the owner can be located at the address listed in the copyright registration), or an authorized reproducing service."

10. For the text and manner of display of this notice, see Appendix B.

11. See Appendix B for the placement of this notice on the interlibrary loan form.

12. This search would have to include at least checking with the publisher and the well known reprint agents. House Report (Judiciary Committee) No.94-1476, Sept. 3, 1976 [To accompany S.22] states on page 76: "The scope and nature of a reasonable investigation to determine that an

unused copy cannot be obtained will vary according to the circumstances of a particular situation. It will always require recourse to commonly-known trade sources in the United States, and in the normal situation also to the publisher or other copyright owner (if the owner can be located at the address listed in the copyright registration), or an authorized reproducing service."

13. See Appendix B for the text and exact wording required for this warning sign.

6
Audio and Video Tapes

- *Can I use my own personal copy of the video* Roots *to show to my eighth grade class as part of our Black History Week studies? It has an FBI warning on it.*

- *The National Organization for Women meets regularly in our public library's community room. We don't control what kinds of videotapes they show. Should we?*

- *As a School Library Media Specialist, I have purchased equipment for the school library that makes it possible for me to edit videotapes and to combine two or more into a montage. That's okay, isn't it?*

- *The director of the local senior center often comes into our public library and borrows videotapes that we suspect she's showing to a group of seniors. Is that all right? If not, should we stop her from borrowing the tapes?*

BASIC PRINCIPLES

With audio and video materials, as with printed matter, it is important to be aware of what rights accrue to you as the purchaser of

78

a copyrighted work. When you purchase a videotape, for example, you own the physical object. You can do whatever you want with that particular videotape. You can keep it or you can give it away. You can throw it into the trash, unravel it, jump on it, or run it over with your car. You can lend it to a friend, rent it out, or resell it. But you can't copy it. The right to make copies, with certain exceptions, rests with the copyright owner.

With audio and video materials, as with printed materials, it is always possible to seek the permission of the copyright holder to make copies or to use copyrighted materials in a way that would not normally be permitted. If permission is granted in writing, whether free or for a fee, be sure to stay carefully within the boundaries stated in the written permission.

There will be times when it is not feasible to obtain permission from a copyright holder to make use of audio or video material. The remainder of this chapter will deal with such situations.

Audiotapes

In dealing with audiotapes, the best course is to treat them as if they were printed materials. This advice derives from the copyright law itself, which talks routinely about "copies or phonorecords." Phonorecords are defined as "material objects in which sounds, other than those accompanying a motion picture or other audiovisual work, are fixed by any method now known or later developed, and from which the sounds can be perceived, reproduced, or otherwise communicated, either directly or with the aid of a machine or device." The term "phonorecords" includes the material object in which the sounds are first fixed. This definition seems to embody all of the audio formats, everything from phonograph records and audiotapes, to compact discs, laser disks, and technologies not yet invented. For further guidance in dealing with audiotapes, look to the chapter on printed materials for the concepts embodied in fair use (Section 107) as well as the special exceptions extended to libraries and archives in Section 108.

Videotapes

While audiotapes come under the general category of "phonorecords," videotapes have been given special treatment, primarily because court cases have led to a refinement of the rules for their use.

Videotapes have become a common part of the collections of

libraries and schools. This widespread use has raised many questions about proper practices regarding videotape copying and use. This section explains how to get maximum usage from a videotape while staying within the prescribed guidelines.

Videotapes are sometimes leased or licensed. In these situations, always read the conditions of the lease or license before agreeing to it. Don't take the word of the salesperson, no matter how well-meaning and sincere that person may seem, as to what the lease or license does and doesn't allow. Take the time to read the document yourself, or better yet, have it looked at by legal counsel. Ask questions if the meaning of a particular clause is unclear to you. Be sure that you can honestly live within the boundaries of the lease or license.

Purchased or recorded-off-the-air videos are the main focus of this section. Video prices have reached such a reasonable level that it is now the rule, rather than the exception, for libraries, schools, and consortia to purchase videotapes. With the proliferation of videocassette recorders (VCRs), many people are now able to capture programs they can't watch at the time they are broadcast. The courts call this process "time-shifting."

When one purchases a videotape, there are certain rights that come with it, and others that *may* come with it if certain conditions exist. While there are many variables with purchased videotapes—from the width of a tape to the type of material contained on it—the different rights that come with their purchase are of the most importance to libraries and schools. The two main categories of purchased videotapes are:

· videotapes with public performance rights;
· videotapes for home use only.

Videotapes that are purchased with public performance rights may be played in public and pose no copyright problem for libraries and schools. Videotapes that display the warning that they are intended for home use only are the ones that can pose copyright problems.

Remember, getting the permission of the copyright holder to show a videotape publicly is a legitimate course of action. Get the permission in writing, whether free or for a fee. If there is no time to seek that permission or if a lease or rental with public performance rights is not available, remember that both Section 107 (Fair Use) and Section 108 (Reproduction and Distribution by Libraries and Archives) rights are available under certain circumstances. In addition, broad privileges for educational use of videotapes in the classroom are extended under Section 110 of the Copyright Law.

Classroom Use of Purchased Videotapes

First, let's consider the classroom. The classroom teacher has been given some extremely valuable privileges in regard to the use of home-use only videos. There are conditions that allow the use of these tapes in a classroom setting, giving teachers a distinct advantage.

Classroom conditions for the use of a copyrighted videotape include:

1. The teaching must be face-to-face.
2. The use must take place in a nonprofit educational institution.
3. It must take place in a classroom or similar place devoted to instruction.
4. The videotape must have been lawfully made and the person responsible must have had no reason to believe it was made unlawfully.

Further stipulations are that the use must be by the instructor, a guest instructor, or an enrolled member of the class. Face-to-face teaching implies that the class and teacher are either all together or can see each other somehow, perhaps via distance learning technology. It also implies that the video is related to the class curriculum and is not simply an entertainment for the class. All of these conditions must be met to qualify for an exemption to the "home use only" rule.

It's easy to see that these conditions rule out a rainy-day showing of a "home use only" video in the school cafeteria or auditorium. This is the place where a video with public performance rights is needed. Usually the videos with public performance rights are more expensive than those without, but they must be used in situations where the performance could be construed as "public."

Teachers often ask if a youngster who was absent on the day a video was shown to the class can view it another time. The answer is yes. The showing, in that case, could take place in a quiet corner of the classroom, or the video could be lent for viewing at home. A carrel in the school library might be another good place for this "catch-up" activity also, assuming that the school library is used for systematic instructional activities. As a matter of fact, even nonclass members can borrow the tape for home viewing.

Classroom Use of Off-the-Air Videotapes

While the rules above apply to purchased videotapes, there are some special guidelines that have been developed, under the fair use doctrine, that make it possible for a teacher personally to record a program or to request that a videotape be made directly off-the-air for use in the classroom. Certain restrictions apply. These are:

1. The educational institution must be nonprofit.
2. The educational institution is expected to establish procedures intended to maintain the integrity of the guidelines established for the classroom use of off-air videotapes.
3. The recording or request for recording as well as the actual use of the tape must be made by an individual teacher.
4. The request for recording may be made of and carried out by the school library media specialist on school library media center equipment or any other unit of the system designated to fulfill such requests under established procedures.
5. Off-air recordings cannot be regularly made in anticipation of possible requests.
6. The recording must include the copyright notice as broadcast.
7. Recording of a program off-air can be done or requested only once by the same teacher no matter how many times it is broadcast.
8. The use must take place in a classroom or similar place devoted to instruction.
9. The classroom or similar place of instruction must be within a single building, cluster or campus, or in the home of a student receiving formalized home instruction.
10. The videotape may be viewed, in whole or in part, only once by each class in the course of relevant teaching activities.
11. The videotape may be viewed again once if instructional reinforcement is needed.
12. Both the original and repeat performances of the videotape must take place within 10 consecutive school session days from the day of the recording. (Vacations, weekends, holidays, exam periods, etc., do not count.)
13. The videotape must be destroyed or erased within 45 consecutive calendar days after the recording.
14. After the classroom use period of 10 consecutive school days has passed, the off-air videotape may be used through the remainder of the 45-consecutive-calendar-days retention period only for teacher evaluation as to its value to the curriculum, for the purpose of possible purchase.
15. The original contents of the off-air recorded program cannot be altered, or combined or merged with other recordings.
16. Subject to all of the above guidelines, a limited number of copies of an off-air videotape may be made to meet the legitimate needs of individual teachers.

In our workshops on copyright, we often are told by school library media specialists that teachers want to retain off-air videotapes for use during the next semester or next year. In fact, teachers often request that the tapes be retained for further use in the school library. That is clearly a violation of the copyright law and the guidelines developed for classroom use of off-air videotapes. School media specialists who receive such requests should do two things— say no (politely) and make sure that all teachers have a copy of the guidelines for classroom use of off-air videotapes.

Libraries and Videotapes

Libraries and their patrons always have the benefit of the privileges extended under the doctrine of fair use (Section 107 of the U.S. Copyright Law). Libraries, as institutions that meet the criteria of Section 108 (Reproduction by Libraries and Archives), are accorded certain additional special privileges. Under these two sections of the law, there are limitations placed on the exclusive rights of the copyright holder that may allow libraries to use videotapes in ways that would otherwise be prohibited.

School and academic libraries are the only libraries that have systematic instructional activities that would qualify them to make and use videotapes made off-air from broadcast programs for classroom use. This privilege does not extend to special or public libraries, unless they are being used as instructional facilities meeting all of the guidelines established for classroom use of off-air videotapes.

There are two categories of videotape usage that are of particular interest to libraries:

1. Videotapes that are available as part of the collection for loan to patrons.
2. Videotapes that are played in the library for one reason or another.

A videotape that is intended only for home use can be lent to library patrons. That is part of what comes with acquiring the physical object—the ability to loan, rent, or resell it at all. Some basic rules apply:

1. All types of libraries may lend videotapes intended for home use to patrons for personal use.
2. Such loans may or may not include a reasonable fee.
3. Any copyright notice on a videotape should be left unobstructed.
4. Such videotapes should not be lent knowingly to a group for a public performance.
5. Patrons who wish to borrow such tapes for public performance should be informed that such use may be unlawful, although the library does not have a duty to withhold the material.
6. If library equipment is available for loan for the playing of home-use-

only videotapes, such equipment should carry a warning that many videotapes are protected under copyright law, which prohibits unauthorized copying.

Now what about the issue of playing videotapes in the library itself? Well, we already know two things about that subject. One is that tapes with public performance rights can be viewed just about anywhere, and that includes in any type of library. The second is that school libraries or media centers are generally recognized as instruction centers, so both public performance tapes and "for home viewing only" tapes may be viewed there, with the home-only type to be used in the regular course of instruction.

Now it's time to consider the public library. Public libraries today often feature both adult and children's programs. Certainly, for some of these programs, there are videotapes that enhance the subject being presented. If these videotapes are for home viewing only, a public library cannot use them in a program presented to the public, unless, of course, the written permission of the copyright holder is obtained or the videotape is leased or licensed for the specific purpose of a public performance. Without that permission, lease, or license, a showing in a library's public space would be a copyright infringement. This is true when the showing is free as well as when a fee is charged. If a fee is charged, it should be small and related to the maintenance of the videotape or the playing equipment.

Public libraries usually have rooms that they allow groups to use, sometimes for a fee and sometimes free. To be safe, the library should have an agreement, signed by the group's agent, that includes a clause stating that the group will only show videotapes that are properly licensed or have public performance rights and a clause that holds the library harmless if the group fails to comply.

Even permitting public library patrons to view home-use-only videotapes individually and privately can have its pitfalls, since the possibility exists that a group of unrelated persons could assemble by accident, constituting a public performance. It is better for the library to lend the videotapes for use outside the library, even if the equipment to play the tapes must also be provided.

All video playing equipment owned by the library, even that which is intended to be used only in-house, should carry the warning that many videotapes are protected by copyright and that unauthorized copying is prohibited by law.

It is possible for a public library space to be used as a classroom with enrolled students and a designated instructor. In such cases, the use of a for-home-use-only videotape should not be an infringement if all the other classroom conditions stipulated above are met.

Finally, there is the issue of making copies of videotapes, in part or in whole. This question can be answered using the rules that apply to photocopying under Section 107 (Fair Use) and Section 108 (Reproduction by Libraries and Archives), which are explained in Chapter 5.

CASE STUDY

Your public library has been offered the gift of a large-screen television with a built-in VCR for the children's department. The grandmotherly lady making the offer says that she thinks it would be so nice if the children who come in could watch movies like *Pinocchio* and *The Little Mermaid* together. You haven't had any experience with this kind of situation, but you know that there are copyright implications. If you take the offer of the gift, what can the children watch without infringing on a copyright?

ANSWER: From your reading, you know that the videos that can be watched by the public are those that have public performance rights or for which you get permission.

7

Music

- *If there are not enough copies of music for the whole high school band, is it okay to make copies?*

- *Is it okay to improve the arrangement of the piece?*

- *Can we put our own words to a melody that has none?*

- *Can our class broadcast the musical comedy we've done for parents over our local access cable channel?*

- *May I record the performances of my music students?*

BASIC PRINCIPLES

At the same time that a group of interested parties was developing guidelines for classroom copying in a not-for-profit educational institution, another group was working on guidelines for the educational use of music.

As with any copyrighted material, when one wishes to copy, modify, or otherwise embellish printed music, the first course of action is to seek permission from the copyright holder. Permissions should always be in writing. There may be a fee to obtain such permission. Fees are generally negotiable. When there are time constraints or other good reasons for not getting permission, there are limited privileges that allow certain normally prohibited activities in special circumstances.

Representatives of the Music Publishers' Association of the United States, Inc., the Music Teachers National Association, the Music Education National Conference, the National Association of Schools of Music, and the Ad Hoc Committee on Copyright Law Revision met and developed permissible uses regarding printed music. These guidelines state the minimum, not the maximum, standards of educational fair use (Section 107 of the U.S. Copyright Act) in effect at the present time. Over time, the conditions that determine the extent of permissible copying for educational purposes may change, making certain types of copying now permitted impermissible in the future and, conversely, making presently impermissible copying possible. It is, therefore, important for library staff members to keep current on developments in this area of the law. Usually, the commonly-read professional journals will carry news of changes in the copyright law that affect libraries and schools.

There also may be instances in which copying that doesn't fall within the guidelines shown below may nonetheless be permitted under the criteria of fair use, so it is advisable to know these criteria and to check with legal counsel if there is doubt as to the advisability of a particular course of action.

Educational Uses of Music

The guidelines for permissible uses as developed by the representatives of the groups described above allow for the following educational uses of music:

1. Emergency copying to replace purchased copies that for any reason are not available for an *imminent* performance, *provided that purchased replacement copies shall be substituted in due course.*
2. For academic purposes other than performance, multiple copies of excerpts of works may be made, provided that the excerpts do not comprise a part of the whole that would constitute a performable unit such as a section, movement or aria, *but* in no case more than 10 percent of the whole work (the number of copies shall not exceed one copy per pupil).
3. For academic purposes other than performance, a single copy of an entire performable unit (section, movement, aria, etc.) that is:
   - confirmed by the copyright proprietor to be out of print, or
   - unavailable except in a larger work

may be made by or for a teacher *solely* for the purpose of his or her scholarly research or in preparation to teach a class.

4. For academic purposes other than performance, printed copies that have been purchased may be edited or simplified provided that:
   - the fundamental character of the work is not distorted, or
   - the lyrics, if any, are not altered, or lyrics are not added if none exist.
5. A single copy of recordings of performances by students may be made for evaluation or rehearsal purposes and may be retained by the educational institution or individual teacher.
6. A single copy of a sound recording such as a tape, disc, or cassette of copyrighted music may be made from sound recordings owned by an educational institution or an individual teacher for the purpose of constructing aural exercises or examinations and may be retained by the educational institution or individual teacher. This proviso pertains only to the copyright of the music itself and not to any copyright that may exist in the sound recording.

While these permissible uses seem to be expressed in a straightforward way, note that in the first item the key term "in due course" is an undefined time period in which "purchased replacement copies shall be substituted" for the emergency copies made for an imminent performance. Because of this lack of definition, the best advice that can be given is that the phrase "in due course" should be interpreted as meaning "as quickly as possible."

In the third item above, there is the odd requirement that the "copyright proprietor," another undefined term that probably means "copyright holder," must confirm that a piece of music is out of print before the single copy of an entire performable unit is made. Presumably, the fact that the material is out of print would be located through standard—to librarians—reference works and then confirmed as indicated.

Another important but undefined term appears in the fourth item. The editing allowed in that permissible use is only that which does not distort the "fundamental character" of the work. Since there is no definition for "fundamental character," the safest course is to edit minimally, if at all.

There are general prohibitions that exist in conjunction with the guidelines. These are:

1. The copying may *not* be used to create, replace, or substitute for anthologies, compilations, or collective works.
2. The copying may not be of or from works intended to be "consumable" in the course of study or of teaching, such as workbooks, exercises, standardized tests and answer sheets, and like material.

3. Copying for the purpose of performance is prohibited, except in the emergency situation described above.
4. Copying as a way of avoiding purchase is forbidden, given the reasonable availability of the material.
5. No copying is permitted without the copyright notice that appears on the printed music.

Musical Performances

While the issues surrounding the copying of sheet music are important ones, there are additional copyright questions that come up regarding the performance of the music. The public performance of music is a copyright infringement unless there is a license to perform. Certain performances of music in schools and libraries, however, because of the rights given by Section 110 of the Copyright law, are not infringements. Here's how that works:

In a nonprofit educational institution, in the course of face-to-face teaching activities, in a classroom or similar place devoted to instruction, instructors or pupils may perform or display a work—*unless*, in the case of a motion picture or other audiovisual work, the performance, or the display of individual images, is given by means of a copy that was not lawfully made, and the person responsible for the performance knew or had reason to believe it was not lawfully made.

In addition, the following are not infringements of copyright:

1. Performance of a nondramatic literary or musical work or display of a work, by or in the course of a transmission, if:
   • the performance or display is a regular part of the systematic instructional activities of a governmental body or a nonprofit educational institution, and
   • the performance or display is directly related and of material assistance to the teaching content of the transmission, and
   • the transmission is made primarily for: reception in classrooms or similar places normally devoted to instruction; reception by persons to whom the transmission is directed because their disabilities or other special circumstances prevent their attendance in classrooms or similar places normally devoted to instruction; or reception by officers or employees of governmental bodies as a part of their official duties or employment.
2. Performance of a nondramatic literary or musical work otherwise than in a transmission to the public, without any purpose of direct or indirect commercial advantage and without payment of any fee or

other compensation for the performance to any of its performers, promoters, or organizers, if:

- There is no direct or indirect admission charge, or
- The proceeds, after deducting the reasonable costs of producing the performance, are used exclusively for educational, religious, or charitable purposes, and not for private financial gain, except where the copyright owner has served notice of objection to the performance under the following conditions:

  i. the notice shall be in writing and signed by the copyright owner or such owner's duly authorized agent

  ii. the notice shall be served on the person responsible for the performance at least seven days before the date of the performance, and shall state the reasons for the objection

  iii. the notice shall comply, in form, content and manner of service, with requirements that the Register of Copyrights shall prescribe by regulation.

Copying of Sheet Music in Libraries

As with other formats of copyrighted materials, libraries have the privileges extended under both fair use (Section 107) and the Section 108 privileges of reproduction by libraries and archives. Examine the guidelines for printed materials as presented in Chapter 5 above should a question arise in regard to either sheet music or phonorecordings.

CASE STUDY

You are the school library media specialist at the local high school. The music department head, Jim Burton, is a good friend of yours. Jim's attitude, with regard to the copying of music for his students and for himself, is that no one is ever going to sue a school. Consequently, he freely copies whatever he wishes.

In addition, Jim is very good at making up light-hearted poems of the sort known as "doggerel." He has decided to make up a set of "fun" lyrics to the theme from the movie *Superman* to be performed at the graduation ceremony this June.

Jim says to you, "Do a little research for me, and see how I can do this in such a way that there's no problem. There must be a loophole for teachers, making it possible for them to do a nice thing like this for their students."

You agree to look up the law to see if what Jim wants to do is allowed? Is it? If it is allowed, are there criteria that must be met? What would you advise Jim to do?

Answer: Don't advise Jim but do give him a copy of the guidelines for the use of music in a nonprofit educational institution. His questions may be answered there. If not, he should consult an attorney.

FULL TEXT

Guidelines for Educational Uses of Music

The purpose of the following guidelines is to state the minimum and not the maximum standards of educational fair use under Section 107 of H.R. 2223. The parties agree that the conditions determining the extent of permissible copying for educational purposes may change in the future; that certain types of copying permitted under these guidelines may not be permissible in the future, and conversely that in the future other types of copying not permitted under these guidelines may be permissible under revised guidelines.

Moreover, the following statement of guidelines is not intended to limit the types of copying permitted under the standards of fair use under judicial decision and which are stated in Section 107 of the Copyright Revision Bill. There may be instances in which copying which does not fall within the guidelines stated below may nonetheless be permitted under the criteria of fair use.

A. Permissible Uses

1. Emergency copying to replace purchased copies which for any reason are not available for an imminent performance provided purchased replacement copies shall be substituted in due course.
2. a) For academic purposes other than performance, multiple copies of excerpts of works may be made, provided that the excerpts do not comprise a part of the whole which would constitute a performable unit such as a section, movement or aria, but in no case more than 10% of the whole work. The number of copies shall not exceed one copy per pupil.

   b) For academic purposes other than performance, a single copy of an entire performable unit (section, movement, aria, etc.) that is. (1) confirmed by the copyright proprietor to be out of print, or (2) unavailable except in a larger work, may be made by or for a teacher solely for the purpose of his or her scholarly research or in preparation to teach a class.
3. Printed copies which have been purchased may be edited or simplified provided that the fundamental character of the work is not distorted or the lyrics, if any, altered or lyrics added if none exist.
4. A single copy of recordings of performances by students may be made for evaluation or rehearsal purposes and may be retained by the educational institution or individual teacher.
5. A single copy of a sound recording (such as a tape, disc or cassette) of copyrighted music may be made from sound recordings owned by an educational institution or an individual teacher for the purpose of

constructing aural exercises or examinations and may be retained by the educational institution or individual teacher. (This pertains only to the copyright of the music itself and not to any copyright which may exist in the sound recording.)

B. Prohibitions

1. Copying to create or replace or substitute for anthologies, compilations or collective works.
2. Copying of or from works intended to be "consumable" in the course of study or of teaching such as workbooks, exercises, standardized tests and answer sheets and like material.
3. Copying for the purpose of performance, except A(1) above.
4. Copying for the purpose of substituting for the purchase of music except as in A(1) and A(2) above.
5. Copying without the inclusion of the copyright notice which appears on the printed copy.

8

Unique Problems of Academic and Special Libraries

- *Do academic libraries need to restrict access to their manuscript collections?*

- *Could a corporation library get into trouble just for photocopying one article from a journal?*

- *How have recent court decisions affected interlibrary loans between academic libraries?*

Academic and special libraries have special problems complying with the copyright law. These problems are in addition to those encountered by other libraries and result from their unique collections or from the ways in which they must conduct their business. For academic libraries these problems revolve around three areas:

1. manuscript collections
2. reserve collections
3. interlibrary loans.

In special libraries, these problems have to do with the photocopying of articles from newsletters and journals—particularly in for-profit institutions.

Some recent court decisions have raised the concerns of many academic and special librarians about these issues. This chapter focuses on these cases and their implications for all academic and special libraries.

ACADEMIC LIBRARIES

The two recent court rulings on copyright issues that have raised concerns in academic libraries are *Salinger* v. *Random House, Inc.*[1] (generally called the *Salinger* case) and *Basic Books, Inc.* v. *Kinko's Graphics Corp.* (known as the *Kinko* case).[2]

Management of Manuscript Collection

The *Salinger* case raises several concerns for academic librarians particularly about providing access to their manuscript collections. In this 1987 case, Ian Hamilton, a respected writer, wrote a manuscript for a biography of novelist J.D. Salinger. Hamilton quoted and paraphrased some letters written by Salinger to a number of people, who, without Mr. Salinger's knowledge, had deposited these letters in several universities' libraries. Random House intended to publish the manuscript. When Mr. Salinger became aware of the use of the letters in the manuscript, he indicated his displeasure. The biographer subsequently reduced the amount of material quoted as well as the amount of material paraphrased. Despite this reduction in the number of direct quotes and paraphrases, Salinger still protested and ultimately went to court to enjoin publication of the biography. Hamilton claimed that his was a "fair use" of the Salinger documents. When Salinger lost the case at the trial court level, he appealed. The appeal court found in Salinger's favor.

There were three universities (Harvard, Princeton, and the University of Texas) involved in the Salinger case, each of which had written agreements that made it clear that to use the materials in question, a researcher was required to obtain permission from both the literary copyright holder and the university. Hamilton signed that agreement.

In its ruling, the appeals court gave heavy weight to the fact that the letters were unpublished; that is, that they had not been distributed voluntarily to the public by the author. In addition, the court gave great weight to the fact that, because Salinger remained the owner of the contents of the letters, even though the physical documents belonged to those to whom he had written the letters, Salinger might one day choose to publish them for profit. The outcome of the case has caused a good deal of consternation on the part of academic librarians. They worry about who should use similar materials that are deposited in their own libraries, and for what purpose.

Before dealing with these questions as copyright issues, academic librarians should remember that materials donated to university libraries sometimes are given only after certain conditions are imposed. For example, a deceased former United States senator's papers are in a library collection but, for the present, may only be accessed with the permission of the senator's son. It is important for staff in a library to be familiar with any agreements of this kind.

In addition to the constraints agreed to by a college or university in accepting unpublished works such as letters, papers, or manuscripts, it is important to note that the physical transfer of such documents to a new location, such as a college library, does not mean that the bundle of rights granted by the copyright law go with the item. In other words, the university or college does not automatically get the copyright to a work when a gift is made. This only happens if the copyright owner stipulates as much.[3] While this fact is one that is commonly understood for a published item that is purchased, there seems to be some confusion over this issue when an unpublished item is donated.

Furthermore, since copyright is a "bundle" of rights—the right to reproduce a work, to distribute a work to the public, to perform it in public, to display it in public, and to make derivative works—it is possible for an academic library to be given none, some, or all of the rights within this "bundle." An example of this situation is the common one in which an author grants a publisher the right to print and distribute a work, but keeps the reproduction and derivation rights for himself or herself.

Now to the question that academic librarians ask after becoming aware of the *Salinger* decision—that is, "What does this decision mean for our manuscript (or letter or private papers) collection? Should we restrict its use in some new way?" Let's assume that the library is adhering closely to any agreement with the donors restricting the use of such collections. Now, let's turn to copyright law concerns. If the library has received the copyright with the material, then it can grant or withhold permission to use the materials. For example, permission might be given by the university or college to a requestor to quote from a manuscript with or without restriction. On the other hand, if the university or college library does not own the copyright, then an author should seek the permission of the copyright holder to quote from the material. The academic library holding the material may make a rule, to protect itself, that materials deposited with it cannot be quoted or paraphrased, copied, or published without the written permission of the copyright holder. Some universities insist that the holding library must also give its permission. A form to be signed by researchers agreeing to the requirement for written permission(s) should be developed under the supervision of an attorney, since the library will want to be protected fully if there is litigation.

A library might take the stance that the onus of copyright infringement is on the user. To protect itself, the library may require researchers using manuscripts, private papers, and letters to sign a form, again best developed by an attorney, holding the library harmless should a problem arise. Under such circumstances, a researcher who cannot contact the copyright holder, or who has no time to do so, might choose to paraphrase or quote parts of a work under the rubric of fair use. With proper library safeguards in place, the course of action that a researcher decides to take is his or her own responsibility. An objection to the course of action taken by a user in regard to the use of an item is the responsibility of the copyright holder.

The library may maintain a file of the names and addresses of copyright holders for the materials in question if such information is known. If the author has registered with the U.S. copyright office, that office can provide information on the copyright holder (including information on the transfer of copyright by the holder). Because manuscripts, letters, and papers are unpublished and often unregistered, the copyright office may not have the requested information. In that case, a library can explore whether or not the author is still living, and, if deceased, the death date. A living author can then be contacted directly to inquire about copyright status. A deceased author's executor or heirs may be contacted to ascertain the status of copyright. Alternatively, the donor of an item, if the donor is not the author or an author's heir(s), may be the source for information on who holds the copyright. If pertinent information about the dates of creation of an item or the death of an author are not obtainable, the best assumption that a library can make is that a living author or the heirs of a deceased author do hold a copyright in the material in question. Finally, while there is no legal requirement to do so, as a matter of courtesy a library might wish to notify the author or other appropriate party that the materials are in its collection. (Remember, Mr. Salinger had not been aware, prior to the use by Hamilton of the contents, that the letters he had written to his friends were now in three university libraries.)

A case that looks similar to *Salinger*, except for its outcome, should be noted here to illustrate the fact that similar sets of circumstances can result in quite different conclusions by the courts. The case, *Wright* v. *Warner Books, Inc.* (known as *Wright* case), involved the attempt by the late author Richard Wright's widow to enjoin the further distribution of the scholarly biography of Wright, written by academician Margaret Walker. Two publishers refused to publish the biography, entitled *Richard Wright: Daemonic Genius*, after Ellen Wright refused permission for the paraphrasing of both the published and unpublished works of her late husband. Warner Books, the third house to consider the work, decided to go ahead with its publication.

In this case, the court found fair use. The courts distinguished this case from *Salinger*, saying that Walker's use of the materials from Wright "enhanced her analysis and added to her credibility." The court also noted that Walker was a friend of the writer and had a unique insight into his career. In weighing the four factors that constitute fair use, the appeals court said that:

1. The purpose and character of the biography's use of the letters and journal entries was scholarly and favored the defendant (Walker/ Warner).
2. The nature of the copyrighted work—unpublished— favored the plaintiff (Wright).
3. The amount and substantiality of the portions used in relation to the copyrighted work as a whole was small and enhanced the final work. This favored Walker/Warner.
4. The effect on the potential market favored the defendant. The court found that Walker's biography "did not pose a significant threat to the potential market for Wright's letters or journals."

While it is important to be aware of the *Wright* case, that case does not change the need for library safeguards, such as the signing of an agreement by a researcher to obtain the copyright holder's permission for the use of works held by a library. What the Wright case does do is show that the courts will undoubtedly continue to be called on to resolve the issue of fair use on a case-by-case basis, with even small differences in fact patterns having the potential to change an outcome.

Reserve Collections

The second case that has generated interest among academic librarians is the 1991 case *Basic Books, Inc.* v. *Kinko's Graphics Corporation* (known as *Kinko*). Kinko copy shops were making copies of excerpts from the plaintiff publishers' books, compiling these into anthologies, and selling them to university students. Kinko neither sought permission from the publishers nor paid any fees to them.

The publishers claimed that Kinko's practices resulted in copyright infringement. Kinko's Graphics Corporation raised the defense of fair use for educational purposes under Section 107 of the U.S. copyright law.

In determining whether or not Kinko's activities were protected by the fair use doctrine, the court looked at the four established factors:

1. The purpose and character of the use, including whether such use is of a commercial nature or is for non-profit educational purposes.
2. The nature of the copyrighted work.
3. The amount and substantiality of the portion used in relation to the copyrighted work as a whole.
4. The effect of the use upon the potential market for or value of the copyrighted work.

The court found that Kinko's Graphics Corporation was a copyright infringer after concluding that Kinko simply repackaged the plaintiffs' works as "course packs" and that Kinko's sole motive was monetary gain rather than the educational advancement motive offered as a defense. In addition, the court determined that Kinko's actions made serious inroads into the profitability of the publishers textbook business.

The court also studied the copy shop's activity in relation to the "Agreement on Guidelines for Classroom Copying in Not-for-Profit Educational Institutions." Since those guidelines specifically state that " . . . Copying shall not be used to create or to replace or substitute for anthologies, compilations or collective works . . . ," it is not surprising that the court decided in favor of the plaintiff publishers.

What does the *Kinko* case mean for academic libraries and librarians? It is too soon to tell, but there are some indicators of which librarians should be aware. In the explanation surrounding the court's decision in *Kinko*, there are several specific references to the fact that Kinko's commercial copying is in contrast to library copying, which may be undertaken under both Sections 107 and 108. That is not to say that libraries should ignore the outcome of *Kinko*. Academic librarians should review the requirements of both pertinent sections of the law to assure that there is compliance, but there seems to be no reason to panic at this point.

This is especially true in light of the fact that the Copyright Clearance Center has established an Anthology Permission Service to process permissions and collect royalty payments from that part of the educational market, including academic departments, bookstores, and copy centers interested in reproducing published material in customized anthologies. Because of the high demand for the service, the CCC admits that its turnaround time is longer than desirable, but predicts an improvement. The service is also hampered to some degree by the fact that not all publishers have joined the request program.

Publishers who are not part of the CCC program, however, may be a part of the PUBNET permissions program. This program, offered through the Association of American Publishers, offers college bookstores and professors the possibility of electronically requesting permission directly from the publisher to use copyrighted items for customized course anthologies. If these avenues for obtaining permission to copy materials do not work for some professors, it is certainly possible that they will turn to their academic libraries for help. If that happens, libraries should review the pertinent sections of the copyright law for guidance in regard to copying and should take care not to exceed the privileges extended therein.

One area of the academic library that might be affected by the *Kinko* ruling is reserves. If a professor is not able to obtain the appropriate permissions in a timely fashion, an alternative approach could be to place the identified materials on reserve. In that case, it is to be expected that some students will copy some of the materials. Most academic libraries have coin-operated, unsupervised copy machines in place for the use of students. Such machines should carry the copyright notice as specified in the law. Then the responsibility for adhering to the law rests with the student.

Interlibrary Loans

Another library operation that the *Kinko* ruling could affect is interlibrary loan. While monographic materials may be borrowed without limits, depending on availability, whole serial issues are seldom lent. Generally, a request for serial material is for a copy of a specific article, made for a specific requestor who becomes the owner of the material. With the "Rule of Five" limiting the number of requests that can be made from a single title less than five years old during a calendar year, a request for the same article from a large number of students could present a problem. To avoid violating the law, the library must buy a subscription to the serial or get permission from the copyright holder—with or without paying a fee—once the limit of five requests from one serial title has been reached. The Copyright Clearance Center and the PUBNET permissions services can be used to facilitate the permissions process.

The copyright law, like most laws, continues to evolve through court interpretations and amendments. So far, academic libraries have been conservative in their use of the privileges extended to them under the copyright law, and this caution has insulated them from litigation. Academic libraries should continue to exercise due care in the future.

SPECIAL LIBRARIES

There have been several recent court cases that have raised concerns among special librarians. These cases have concerned the photocopying of articles in for-profit institution libraries. The cases clearly illustrate many of the copyright compliance problems that are faced by librarians in all types of special libraries.

No One Will Find Out?

Washington Business Information, Inc. v. *Collier, Shannon & Scott* (known as the *Collier, Shannon* case) was the first of these cases to bring home the message that publishers were getting serious about enforcing their rights. The case centered around the alleged systematic copying of a newsletter, the *Product Safety Letter*, by a law firm. Although the case did not actually result in a court decision, settlement was widely reported in newspapers[4] and in many professional publications.

It was not, however, the specific details of the case that worried many special librarians. The publisher of the *Product Safety Letter*, Washington Business Information, Inc., had offered a reward to anyone who provided proof of illegal photocopying of its newsletter. The suspicion quickly grew that a disgruntled employee had contacted Washington Business Information, Inc.

The use of a tactic more familiarly associated with the detection of federal crimes such as tax fraud or the dumping of hazardous waste seems to have driven home the point that copyright infringement is a serious federal crime. Moreover, this case directly addressed two arguments often used in the debate about copyright compliance.

Librarians who have attempted to convince their management of the importance of copyright compliance are frequently told, "No one is going to find out anyway. How will they find out what goes on at our photocopier?" This case made it clear that this assumption is no longer valid. The offering of a reward and the promise of anonymity to the whistleblower has raised the stakes, and points out how vulnerable a copyright infringer is to discovery.

This case also brings up another obstacle faced by librarians. In requesting additional funds to pay permission fees, librarians often are confronted with the argument that if publishers were really serious about enforcement, there would be more suits in the courts. The truth is that most suits brought for unauthorized photocopying are usually settled quietly and never get to court. The high cost of litigation and the fact that these cases involve violation of a federal law clearly lead to quick settlement.

There are two important lessons to be learned from the *Collier, Shannon* case:

1. Depending on not getting caught is an unrealistic way to deal with copyright compliance.
2. Copyright infringement cases are going to get a great deal more publicity. Depend upon publishers to be more aggressive about enforcing their claims.

How Much Copying is Too Much?

Two very recent court cases have help define the limitations on fair use—particularly as it applies to special libraries.

Photocopying of an entire issue of a newsletter

The first case was *Pasha Publications, Inc.* v. *Enmark Gas Corporation* (known as the *Pasha* case).[5] The decision was rendered on March 10, 1992, in the Federal District Court in Texas. The case is significant to special librarians because it held that the copying and faxing of an entire newsletter for commercial purposes was not within the fair use exception to the copyright law.

The copying was not done for one of the purposes mentioned in the statute: criticism, comment, news reporting, teaching, scholarship or research.[6] The court's analysis of the four factors used to determine fair use was:

1. Purpose and character of the use. In this case, the use was for a commercial enterprise and the copying was in the furtherance a commercial pursuit.
2. Nature of the copyrighted work. Fair use is narrower in the case of newsletters than for mass circulation periodicals.[7]
3. The amount and substantiality of the portion used in relation to the copyrighted work as a whole. In this case the entire newsletter was photocopied and transmitted by facsimile to a branch office.
4. The effect of the use on the potential market of the copyrighted work. In this case, the copying and faxing rendered it unnecessary to purchase additional subscriptions.

On this basis the court determined that the photocopying was not fair use.

Copying of a single article from a journal

The second case *American Geophysical Union* v. *Texaco, Inc.*[8] *(known hereafter as the Texaco* case) is of particular importance and may prove to be one of the most significant copyright decisions affecting libraries in commercial institutions.

The case is important to special librarians for three reasons:

1. The issue in this case was the making of single copies from a copyrighted journal that the library subscribed to.
2. The photocopying was done for scientists at Texaco either personally or by the library staff.
3. Authorization to photocopy this particular journal was available through the Copyright Clearance Center but was not requested.

Unlike cases that address the issue of the systematic photocopying that might substitute for a subscription, the *Texaco* case considers the copying of a single article. The court's analysis of this case can best be seen in terms of the four standard factors of fair use.

The first factor—the purpose and character of the use—looks at two questions: 1) Is the use of the work to further human knowledge or is it merely to multiply the number of original copies? 2) Is the use noncommercial, for a socially beneficial or widely accepted purpose, or is it to further commercial interests?

In this particular case, the court determined that the first factor favored the publisher of the journal. The use here was done merely to multiply the number of originals. The copies replaced the original and added nothing productive to it. The copying did not create something new or different from the original. In addition, the use was of a commercial nature, not for nonprofit educational purposes.

The second factor is the nature of the purpose for which the work is being copied. In the court's opinion, this factor favored Texaco.[9] Copying of factual works are more likely to be deemed fair use than copying works of fiction since facts cannot be copyrighted.

The third factor looks to the amount and substantiality of the portion used in relation to the copyrighted work as a whole. In this case the entire copyrighted article was copied. This factor favored the publisher.

The fourth factor looks at the effect of the use on the potential market or value of the copyrighted work. The publisher argued that if articles were not photocopied Texaco would have to provide its scientists with more copies either by purchasing more subscriptions or by paying a copying fee through a mechanism such as the Copyright Clearance Center (CCC).

Texaco cited the famous library photocopying case *Williams & Wilkins Co. v. United States*[10] (known as the *Williams & Wilkins* case) in its defense.[11] In that case a major publisher of medical journals sued a federal medical research organization and its library for copyright infringement of four of its journals. The library photocopied articles from medical journals at the request of medical researchers and practitioners. The library restricted copying on individual requests to a single copy of a single article and to articles of less than 50 pages.

The court accepted the arguments of the publisher concerning the effect of the copying upon their market. On the reference to the *Williams & Wilkins* case, the court pointed out that the *Texaco* case was different from the *Williams & Wilkins* case for two reasons:

1. Texaco's photocopying in contrast to *Williams & Wilkins* was done for financial gain.
2. There was financial harm done to the publisher.

The court also pointed out that since the *Williams & Wilkins* case, the CCC has been established, making the argument that science would be harmed if this photocopying were not allowed. In short, the court determined that the fourth factor favored the publisher even though only single articles were copied.

There are several lessons to be learned from the *Texaco* case. First, there are options for special libraries including:

- Photocopying the table of contents or subscribing to reprints of the summary section as part of your subscription.[12] Route these, not the original. Original copies could be kept in the library and sent to patrons upon request. Keeping the original in the library also makes it easier to find the publication without tracking through an entire routing list.
- Where possible, using public domain sources. Remember, publishers cannot claim copyright to materials in the public domain, only to the enhancements they add to them.
- Purchasing additional subscriptions. Most publishers offer substantial discounts for additional subscriptions and if they do not, consider finding a new source for the same information that does offer such a price break.
- Obtaining an original lawfully owned copy through interlibrary loan and using it instead of a photocopy. It is a little more work, but it is legal.
- Asking for permission. Most publishers will grant permission for

limited use of their materials or will provide a low-cost reprint. Some also promise quick turnaround time.
• Utilize the Copyright Clearance Center (CCC).

The CCC offers two basic plans. The Annual Authorization Service (AAS) makes it possible to pay a single annual payment. CCC conducts a survey of your photocopying, makes a projection, and then licenses participants to make as many copies as they need for internal use. CCC arranges for payment of the fees to individual publishers.

AAS offers several advantages: there is little paperwork involved; there is no restriction on the volume of copying; and it is no longer necessary to obtain permission from publishers before copying. The major disadvantage is that not all publishers are CCC participants.

CCC also offers a Transactional Reporting Service (TRS), which allows payment on a per transaction basis. For further information about their services contact CCC at 21 Congress Street, Salem, MA 01970. Their telephone number is (508) 744-3350.

If history has a lesson to teach us it is this: libraries have always been at the forefront of copyright law reform and must continue to be.

Endnotes

1. 811 F.2d 90 (1987).
2. 758 F.Supp. 1522 (1991).
3. For one, 17 U.S.C. § 204 requires that the transfer be in writing and signed by the copyright owner or by the owner's duly authorized agent.
4. See, for example, David Margolick's "At the Bar" column in the law section of the December 6, 1991 issue of *The New York Times*.
5. 22 U.S.P.Q. 2d 1076 (1992).
6. 17 U.S.C. § 107.
7. The opinion quoted House Report (Judiciary Committee) No. 94-1476, Sept. 3, 1976 [to accompany S.22] at p. 73-74: ". . . as a general principle, it seems clear that the scope of the fair use doctrine should be considerably narrower in the case of newsletters than in that of either mass circulation periodicals or scientific journals."
8. 802 F. Supp. 1 (1992).
9. The court also considered the argument that the journals need copyright protection in order to help finance the printing and distribution of their publications. In the court's opinion, this, however, did not outweigh the factual nature of the work.
10. 487 F.2d 1345, *aff'd*, 420 U.S. 376 (1975).
11. *Williams & Wilkins* is discussed in Chapter 3.
12. Several publishers offer subscriptions to their table of contents or summary sheets. As well as forestalling any legal questions, it is sometimes less costly to purchase these than to photocopy them.

Appendix A

EXCLUSIVE RIGHTS OF A COPYRIGHT OWNER

A copyright is a bundle of rights granted to a copyright owner for a limited period of time. These rights are cumulative and may overlap. The rights which constitute a copyright are listed below[1] along with a definition and an explanation of how they can be violated.

It is generally illegal for anyone other than the copyright owner to exercise these rights. For the limitations on these rights see Chapter 5.

Exclusive Right: Reproduction

Definition: The right to produce a material object in which the work is duplicated, transcribed, imitated or simulated in a fixed form from which it can be "perceived, reproduced, or otherwise communicated, either directly or with the aid of a machine or device."

Infringement by: Reproducing it in whole or in any substantial part, and by duplicating it exactly or by imitation or simulation. Wide departures or variations from the copyrighted work would still be an infringement as long as the author's "expression" rather than merely the author's "ideas" are taken.

Exclusive Right: Adaptation

Definition: Right to prepare derivative work such as a translation, musical arrangement, dramatization, fictionalization, motion picture version, sound recording, art reproduction, abridgment, condensation, or any other form in which a work may be recast, transformed, or adapted.

Infringement by: Preparing a derivative work based upon the copyrighted work. Must incorporate a portion of the copyrighted work in some form; for example, a detailed commentary on a work or a programmatic musical composition inspired by a novel would not normally constitute infringements.

Exclusive Right: Publication

Definition: The right to distribute copies or phonorecords of the copyrighted work to the public by sale or other transfer of ownership, or by rental, lease or lending.

Infringement by: Any unauthorized public distribution of copies or phonorecords that were unlawfully made.

Exclusive Right: Performance

Definition: The right to publicly recite, render, play, dance, or act it, either directly or by means of any device or process or, in the case of a motion picture or other audiovisual work, to show its image in any sequence or to make the sounds accompanying it audible. Extends to literary, musical, dramatic, and choreographic works, pantomimes, and motion pictures and other audiovisual works and sound recordings.

Infringement by: Unauthorized public performance[2] whether for or not for profit. Includes not only the initial rendering or showing, but also any further act by which that rendering or showing is transmitted or communicated to the public. Certain performances, in addition to those that are "private," are exempted or given qualified copyright control under sections 107 - 118 of the Copyright law.

Exclusive Right: Display

Definition: The public showing of an original or reproduction of an original work either directly or by means of film, slide, television image, or any other device or process. In addition to the direct showing of a copy, display would include the projection of an image on a screen or other surface by any method, the transmission of an image by electronic or other means, and the showing of an image on a cathode ray tube, or similar viewing apparatus connected with any sort of information storage and retrieval system. With respect to motion pictures and other audiovisual works, display would include showing individual images nonsequentially.

Infringement by: Unauthorized public display.[3] Includes not only initial public display but also acts that transmit or otherwise communicate a display of the work to the public by means of any device or process. Includes all conceivable forms and combinations of wired or wireless communications media, including but by no means limited to radio and television broadcasting. Each and every method by which the images or sounds comprising a display are picked up and conveyed is a "transmission" and if the transmission reaches the public in that form it falls within scope of "display."

Endnotes

1. Definitions are drawn from 17 U.S.C. §101. Limitations are from the House Report (Judiciary Committee) No. 94-1476 September 3, 1976 [To accompany S.22].
2. A performance or display is "public" if it takes place at a place open to the public or at any place where a substantial number of persons outside of a normal circle of a family and its social acquaintances is gathered. Performances in "semipublic" places such as clubs, lodges, factories, summer camps, and schools are "public performances" subject to copyright control. Also, the definition of "publicly" is applicable whether the members of the public capable of receiving the performance or display receive it in the same place or in separate places and at the same time or at different times.
3. See note 2 above.

Appendix B

I. Display Warning of Copyright

[To Be Displayed at Place Where Interlibrary Loan Orders are Taken]

37 CFR § 201.14(b). A Display Warning of Copyright and an Order Warning of Copyright shall consist of a verbatim reproduction of the following notice, printed in such size and form and displayed in such manner as to comply with paragraph (c) of this section:

NOTICE WARNING CONCERNING COPYRIGHT RESTRICTIONS

The copyright law of the United States (Title 17, United States Code) governs the making of photocopies or other reproductions of copyrighted material.

Under certain conditions specified in the law, libraries and archives are authorized to furnish a photocopy or other reproduction. One of these specific conditions is that the photocopy or reproduction is not to be "used for any purpose other than private study, scholarship, or research." If a user makes a request for, or later uses, a photocopy or reproduction for purposes in excess of "fair use," that user may be liable for copyright infringement.

This institution reserves the right to refuse to accept a copying order if, in its judgment, fulfillment of the order would involve violation of copyright law.

37 CFR § 201.14(c).Form and manner of use. (1) A Display Warning of Copyright shall be printed on heavy paper or other durable material in type at least 18 points in size, and shall be displayed prominently, in such manner and location as to be clearly visible, legible, and comprehensible to a casual observer within the immediate vicinity of the place where orders are accepted.

II. Warning of Copyright

[Text of Warning Notice to be Placed on or Near Photocopier]

NOTICE:

THE COPYRIGHT LAW OF THE UNITED STATES (TITLE 17 U.S. CODE) GOVERNS THE MAKING OF PHOTOCOPIES OR OTHER REPRODUCTIONS OF COPYRIGHTED MATERIAL. THE PERSON USING THIS EQUIPMENT IS LIABLE FOR ANY INFRINGEMENT.

Note: there is no specific requirement except that:

. . . such equipment display a notice that the making of a copy may be subject to the copyright law.

17 U.S.C. § 108(f)(1).

Recommended that type be at least 18 points in size.

III. Warning of Copyright for Software Lending by Nonprofit Libraries

Warning: Computer Software Rental Amendments Act of 1989

37 C.F.R. § 201.24 (b). A Warning of Copyright for Software Rental shall consist of a verbatim reproduction of the following notice, printed in such size and form and affixed in such manner as to comply with paragraph (c) of this subsection.

Warning: This Computer Program is Protected under the Copyright Law. Making a copy of this program without permission of the copyright owner is prohibited. Anyone copying this program without permission of the copyright owner may be subject to payment of up to $100,000 damages and, in some cases, imprisonment for up to one year.

37 C.F.R. § 201.24 (c). Form and manner of use. A Warning of Copyright for Software Rental shall be affixed to the package that contains the copy of the computer program, which is the subject of a library loan to patrons, by means of a label cemented, gummed, or otherwise durably attached to the copies or to a box, reel, cartridge, cassette, or other container used as a permanent receptacle for the copy of the computer program. The notice shall be printed in such manner as to be clearly legible, comprehensible, and readily apparent to a casual user of the computer program.

IV. An Order Warning of Copyright

37 C.F.R § 201.14(a)(2). . . . the "Order Warning of Copyright" is to be included on printed forms supplied by certain libraries and archives and used by their patrons for ordering copies or phonorecords.

37 C.F.R § 201.14(b)(2). An Order Warning of Copyright shall be printed within a box located prominently on the order form itself, either on the front side of the form or immediately adjacent to the space calling for the name or signature of the person using the form. The notice shall be printed in type size no smaller than that used predominantly throughout the form, and in no case shall the type size be smaller than 8 points. The notice shall be printed in such manner as to be clearly legible, comprehensible, and readable apparent to a casual reader of the form.

Appendix C

Full Text of Section 108

(a) Notwithstanding the provisions of section 106, it is not an infringement of copyright for a library or archive, or any of its employees acting within the scope of their employment, to reproduce no more than one copy or phonorecord of a work, or to distribute such copy or phonorecord, under the conditions specified by this section, if—

(1) the reproduction or distribution is made without any purpose of direct or indirect commercial advantage;

(2) the collections of the library or archives are (i) open to the public, or (ii) available not only to researchers affiliated with the library or archives or with the institution of which it is a part, but also to other persons doing research in a specialized field; and

(3) the reproduction or distribution of the work includes a notice of copyright.

(b) The rights of reproduction and distribution under this section apply to a copy or phonorecord of an unpublished work duplicated in facsimile form solely for purposes of preservation and security or for deposit for research use in another library or archives of the type described by clause (2) of subsection (a), if the copy or phonorecord reproduced is currently in the collections of the library or archives.

(c) The rights of reproduction under this section apply to a copy or phonorecord of a published work duplicated in facsimile form solely for the purpose of replacement of a copy or phonorecord that is damaged, deteriorating, lost, or stolen, if the library or archives has, after a reasonable effort, determined that an unused replacement cannot be obtained at a fair price.

(d) The rights of reproduction and distribution under this section apply to a copy, made from the collection of a library or archives where the user makes his or her request or from that of another library or archives, of no more than one article or other contribution to a copyrighted collection or periodical issue, or to a copy or phonorecord of a small part of any other copyrighted work, if—

(1) the copy or phonorecord becomes the property of the user, and the library or archives has had no notice that the copy or phonorecord would be used for any purpose other than private study, scholarship, or research; and

(2) the library or archives displays prominently, at the place where orders are accepted, and includes on its order form, a warning of copyright in accordance with requirements that the Register of Copyrights shall prescribe by regulation.

(e) The rights of reproduction and distribution under this section apply to the entire work, or to a substantial part of it, made from the collection of a library or archives where the user makes his or her request or from that of another library or archives, if the library or archives has first determined, on the basis of a reasonable investigation, that a copy or phonorecord of the copyrighted work cannot be obtained at a fair price, if—

(1) the copy or phonorecord becomes the property of the user, and the library or archives has had no notice that the copy or phonorecord would be used for any purpose other than private study, scholarship, or research; and

(2) the library or archives displays prominently, at the place where orders are accepted, and includes on its order form, a warning of copyright in accordance with requirements that the Register of Copyright shall prescribe by regulation.

(f) Nothing in this section—

(1) shall be construed to impose liability for copyright infringement upon a library or archives or its employees for the unsupervised use of reproducing equipment located on its premises: Provided, that such equipment displays a notice that the making of a copy may be subject to the copyright law;

(2) excuses a person who uses such reproducing equipment or who requests a copy or phonorecord under subsection (d) from liability for copyright infringement for any such act, or for any later use of such copy or phonorecord, if it exceeds fair use as provided by section 107.

(3) shall be construed to limit the reproduction and distribution by

lending of a limited number of copies and excerpts by a library or archives of an audiovisual news program, subject to clauses (1), (2), and (3) of subsection (a); or

(4) in any way affects the rights of fair use as provided by section 107, or any contractual obligations assumed at any time by the library or archives when it obtained a copy or phonorecord of a work in its collections.

(g) The rights of reproduction and distribution under this section extend to the isolated and unrelated reproduction or distribution of a single copy or phonorecord of the same material on separate occasions, but do not extend to cases where the library or archives, or its employee—

(1) is aware or has substantial reason to believe that it is engaging in the related or concerted reproduction or distribution of multiple copies or phonorecords of the same material, whether made on one occasion or over a period of time, and whether intended for aggregate use by one or more individuals or for separate use by the individual members of a group; or

(2) engages in the systematic reproduction or distribution of single or multiple copies or phonorecords of material described in subsection (d): Provided, that nothing in this clause prevents a library or archives from participating in interlibrary arrangements that do not have, as their purpose or effect, that the library or archives receiving such copies or phonorecords for distribution does so in such aggregate quantities as to substitute for a subscription to or purchase of such work.

(h) The rights of reproduction and distribution under this section do not apply to a musical work, a pictorial, graphic or sculptural work, or a motion picture or other audiovisual work other than an audiovisual work dealing with news, except that no such limitation shall apply with respect to rights granted by subsections (b) and (c), or with respect to pictorial or graphic works published as illustrations, diagrams, or similar adjuncts to works of which copies are reproduced or distributed in accordance with subsections (d) and (e).

(i) Five years from the effective date of this Act, and at five-year intervals thereafter, the Register of Copyrights, after consulting with representatives of authors, book and periodical publishers, and other owners of copyrighted materials, and with representatives of library users and librarians, shall submit to the Congress a report setting forth the extent to which this section has achieved the intended statutory balancing of the rights of creators, and the needs of users. The report should also describe any problems that may have arisen, and present legislative or other recommendations, if warranted.

Appendix D

I. EXCERPTS FROM SENATE REPORT ON SECTION 108

The following excerpts are reprinted from the 1975 Senate Report on the new copyright law (S. Rep. No. 94-473, pages 67-71). Where the discussions of particular points are generally similar in the two Reports, the passages from the later House Report are reprinted. Where the discussion of particular points is substantially different, passages from both reports are reprinted.

a. Senate Report: Discussion of Libraries and Archives in Profit-Making Institutions

The limitation of section 108 to reproduction and distribution by libraries and archives "without any purpose of direct or indirect commercial advantage" is intended to preclude a library or archives in a profit-making organization from providing photocopies of copyrighted materials to employees engaged in furtherance of the organization's commercial enterprise, unless such copying qualifies as a fair use, or the organization has obtained the necessary copyright licenses. A commercial organization should purchase the number of copies of a work that it requires, or obtain the consent of the copyright owner to the making of the photocopies.

b. Senate Report: Discussion of Multiple Copies and Systematic Reproduction

Subsection (g) provides that the rights granted by this section extend only to the "isolated and unrelated reproduction of a single copy," but this section does not authorize the related or concerted reproduction of multiple copies of the same material whether made on one occasion or over a period of time, and whether intended for

116

aggregate use by one individual or for separate use by the individual members of a group. For example, if a college professor instructs his class to read an article from a copyrighted journal, the school library would not be permitted, under subsection (g), to reproduce copies of the article for the members of the class.

Subsection (g) also provides that section 108 does not authorize the systematic reproduction or distribution of copies or phonorecords of articles or other contributions to copyrighted collections or periodicals or of small parts of other copyrighted works whether or not multiple copies are reproduced or distributed. Systematic reproduction or distribution occurs when a library makes copies of such materials available to other libraries or to groups of users under formal or informal arrangements whose purpose or effect is to have the reproducing library serve as their source of such material. Such systematic reproduction and distribution, as distinguished from isolated and unrelated reproduction or distribution, may substitute the copies reproduced by the source library for subscriptions or reprints or other copies which the receiving libraries or users might other wise have purchased for themselves, from the publisher or the licensed reproducing agencies.

While it is not possible to formulate specific definitions of "systematic copying," the following examples serve to illustrate some of the copying prohibited by subsection (g).

(1) A library with a collection of journals in biology informs other libraries with similar collections that it will maintain and build its own collection and will make copies of articles from these journals available to them and their patrons on request. Accordingly, the other libraries discontinue or refrain from purchasing subscriptions to these journals and fulfill their patrons' requests for articles by obtaining photocopies from the source library.

(2) A research center employing a number of scientists and technicians subscribes to one or two copies of needed periodicals. By reproducing photocopies of articles the center is able to make the material in these periodicals available to its staff in the same manner which otherwise would have required multiple subscriptions.

(3)Several branches of a library system agree that one branch will subscribe to particular journals in lieu of each branch purchasing its own subscriptions, and the one subscribing branch will reproduce copies of articles from the publication for users of the other branches.

The committee believes that section 108 provides an appropriate statutory balancing of the rights of creators, and the needs of users. However, neither a statute nor legislative history can specify precisely which library photocopying practices constitute the making of "single copies" as distinguished from "systematic reproduction." Isolated single spontaneous requests must be distinguished from "systematic reproduction." The photocopying needs of such operations as multi-county regional systems must be met. The committee therefore recommends that representatives of authors, book and periodical publishers and other owners of copyrighted material meet with the library community to formulate photocopying guidelines to assist library patrons and employees. Concerning library photocopying practices not authorized by this legislation, the committee recommends that workable clearance and licensing procedures be developed.

It is still uncertain how far a library may go under the Copyright Act of 1909 in supplying a photocopy of copyrighted material in its collection. The recent case of *Williams and Wilkins Company* v. *The United States* failed to significantly illuminate the application of the fair use doctrine to library photocopying practices. Indeed, the opinion of the Court of Claims said the Court was engaged in "a 'holding operation' in the interim period before Congress enacted its preferred solution."

While the several opinions in the *Wilkins* case have given the Congress little guidance as to the current state of the law on fair use, these opinions provide additional support for the balanced resolution of the photocopying issue adopted by the Senate last year in S. 1361 and preserved in section 108 of this legislation. As the Court of Claims opinion succinctly stated "there is much to be said on all sides."

In adopting these provisions on library photocopying, the committee is aware that through such programs as those of the National Commission on Libraries and Information Science there will be a significant evolution in the functioning and services of libraries. To consider the possible need for changes in copyright law and procedures as a result of new technology, a National Commission on New Technological Uses of Copyrighted Words has been established (Public Law 93-573).

II. EXCERPTS FROM HOUSE REPORT ON SECTION 108

The following excerpts are reprinted from the House Report on the new copyright law (H.R. Rep. No. 94-1476, pages 74-79). All of the Houses Report's discussion of section 108 is reprinted here; similarities and differences between the House and Senate Reports on particular points will be noted below.

a. House Report: Introductory Statement

This paragraph is substantially the same in the Senate and House Report.

Notwithstanding the exclusive rights of the owners of copyright, section 108 provides that under certain conditions it is not an infringement of copyright for a library or archives, or any of its employees acting within the scope of their employment, to reproduce or distribute not more than one copy or phonorecord of a work, provided (1) the reproduction or distribution is made without any purpose of direct or indirect commercial advantage and (2) the collections of the library or archives are open to the public or available not only to researchers affiliated with the library or archives, but also to other persons doing research in a specialized field, and (3) the reproduction or distribution of the work includes a notice of copyright.

b. House Report: Discussion of Libraries and Archives in Profit-making Institutions

The Senate and House Reports differ substantially on this point. The Senate Report's discussion is reprinted above.

Under this provision, a purely commercial enterprise could not establish a collection of copyrighted works, call itself a library or archive, and engage in for-profit reproduction and distribution of photocopies. Similarly, it would not be possible for a non-profit institution, by means of contractual arrangements with a commercial copying enterprise, to authorize the enterprise to carry out copying and distribution functions that would be exempt if conducted by the non-profit institution itself.

The reference to "indirect commercial advantage" has raised questions as to the status of photocopying done by or for libraries or archival collections within industrial, profitmaking, or proprietary institutions (such as the research and development departments of chemical, pharmaceutical, automobile, and oil corporations, the library of a proprietary hospital, the collections owned by a law or medical partnership, etc.).

There is a direct interrelationship between this problem and the prohibitions against "multiple" and "systematic" photocopying in section 108 (g) (1) and (2). Under section 108, a library in a profit-making organization would not be authorized to:

(a) use a single subscription or copy to supply its employees with multiple copies of material relevant to their work; or

(b) use a single subscription or copy to supply its employees, on request, with single copies of material relevant to their work, where the arrangement is "systematic" in the sense of deliberately substituting photocopying for subscription or purchase; or

(c) use "interlibrary loan" arrangements for obtaining photocopies in such aggregate quantities as to substitute for subscriptions or purchase of material needed by employees in their work.

Moreover, a library in a profit-making organization could not evade these obligations by installing reproducing equipment on its premises for unsupervised use by the organization's staff.

Isolated, spontaneous making of single photocopies by a library in a for-profit organization, without any systematic effort to substitute photocopying for subscriptions or purchases, would be covered by section 108, even though the copies are furnished to the employees of the organization for use in their work. Similarly, for-profit libraries could participate in interlibrary arrangements for exchange of photocopies, as long as the reproduction or distribution was not "systematic." These activities, by themselves, would ordinarily not be considered "for direct or indirect commercial advantage," since the "advantage" referred to in this clause must attach to the immediate commercial motivation behind the reproduction or distribution itself, rather than to the ultimate profit-making motivation behind the enterprise in which the library is located. On the other hand, section 108 would not excuse reproduction or distribution if there were a commercial motive behind the actual making or distributing of the copies, if multiple copies were made or distributed, or if the photocopying activities were "systematic" in the sense that their aim was to substitute for subscriptions or purchases.

c. House Report: Rights of Reproduction and Distribution Under Section 108

The following paragraphs are closely similar in the Senate and House Reports.

The rights of reproduction and distribution under section 108 apply in the following circumstances:

Archival reproduction
Subsection (b) authorizes the reproduction and distribution of a copy or phonorecord of an unpublished work duplicated in facsimile form solely for purposes of preservation and security, or for deposit for research use in another library or archives, if the copy of phonorecord

reproduced is currently in the collections of the first library or archives. Only unpublished works could be reproduced under this exemption, but the right would extend to any type of work, including photographs, motion pictures and sound recordings. Under this exemption, for example, a repository could make photocopies of manuscripts by microfilm or electrostatic process, but could not reproduce the work in "machine-readable" language for storage in an information system.

Replacement of damaged copy

Subsection (c) authorizes the reproduction of a published work duplicated in facsimile form solely for the purpose of replacement of a copy or phonorecord that is damaged, deteriorating, lost or stolen, if the library or archives has, after a reasonable effort, determined that an unused replacement cannot be obtained at a fair price. The scope and nature of a reasonable investigation to determine that an unused replacement cannot be obtained will vary according to the circumstances of a particular situation. It will always require recourse to commonly-known trade sources in the United States, and in the normal situation also to the publisher or other copyright owner (if such owner can be located at the address listed in the copyright registration), or an authorized reproducing service.

Articles and small excerpts

Subsection (d) authorizes the reproduction and distribution of a copy of not more than one article or other contribution to a copyrighted collection or periodical issue, or of a copy or phonorecord of a small part of any other copyrighted work. The copy or phonorecord may be made by the library where the user makes his request or by another library pursuant to an interlibrary loan. It is further required that the copy become the property of the user, that the library or archives have no notice that the copy would be used for any purposes other than private study, scholarship or research, and that the library or archives display prominently at the place where reproduction requests are accepted, and includes in its order form, a warning of copyright in accordance with requirements that the Register of Copyrights shall prescribe by regulation.

Out-of-print works

Subsection (e) authorizes the reproduction and distribution of a copy or phonorecord of an entire work under certain circumstances, if it has been established that a copy cannot be obtained at a fair price. The copy may be made by the library where the user makes his request or by another library pursuant to an interlibrary loan. The scope and nature of a reasonable investigation to determine that an unused copy cannot be obtained will vary according to the circumstances of a particular situation. It will always require recourse to commonly-known trade sources in the United States, and in the normal situation also to the publisher or other copyright owner (if the owner can be located at the address listed in the copyright registration), or an authorized reproducing service. It is further required that the copy become the property of the user, that the library or archives have no notice that the copy would be used for any purpose other than private study, scholarship, or research, and that the library or archives display prominently at the place where reproduction requests are accepted, and include on its order form, a warning of copyright in accordance with requirements that the Register of Copyrights shall prescribe by regulation.

d. House Report: General Exemptions for Libraries and Archives

Parts of the following paragraphs are substantially similar in the Senate and House Reports. Differences in the House Report on certain points reflect certain amendments in section 108(f) and elsewhere in the Copyright Act.

General exemptions

Clause (1) of subsection (f) specifically exempts a library or archives or its employees from liability for the unsupervised use of reproducing equipment located on its premises, provided that the reproducing equipment displays a notice that the making of a copy may be subject to the copyright law. Clause (2) of subsection (f) makes clear that this exemption of the library or archives does not extend to the person using such equipment or requesting such copy if the use exceeds fair use. Insofar as such person is concerned the copy or phonorecord made is not considered "lawfully" made for purposes of sections 109, 110 or other provisions of the title.

Clause (3) provides that nothing in section 108 is intended to limit the reproduction and distribution by lending of a limited number of copies and excerpts of an audiovisual news program. This exemption is intended to apply to the daily newscasts of the national television networks, which report the major events of the day. It does not apply to documentary (except documentary programs involving news reporting as that term is used in section 107), magazine-format or other public affairs broadcasts dealing with subjects of general interest to the viewing public.

The clause was first added to the revision bill in 1974 by the adoption of an amendment proposed by Senator Baker. it is intended to permit libraries and archives, subject to the general conditions of this section, to make off-the-air videotape recordings of daily network newscasts for limited distribution to scholars and researchers for use in research purposes. As such, it is an adjunct to the American Television and Radio Archive established in Section 113 of the Act which will be the principal repository for television broadcast material, including news broadcasts. The inclusion of language indicating that such material may only be distributed by lending by the library or archives is intended to preclude performance, copying, or sale, whether or not for profit, by the recipient of a copy of a television broadcast taped off-the-air pursuant to this clause.

Clause (4), in addition to asserting that nothing contained in section 108 "affects the right of fair use as provided by section 107," also provides that the right of reproduction granted by this section does not override any contractual arrangements assumed by a library or archives when it obtains a work for its collections. For example, if there is an express contractual prohibition against reproduction for any purpose, this legislation shall not be construed as justifying a violation of the contract. This clause is intended to encompass the situation where an individual makes papers, manuscripts or other works available to a library with the understanding that they will not be reproduced.

It is the intent of this legislation that a subsequent unlawful use by a user of a copy or phonorecord of a work lawfully made by a library, shall not make the library liable for such improper use.

e. House Report: Discussion of Multiple Copies and Systematic Reproduction

The Senate and House Reports differ substantially on this point. The Senate Report's discussion is reprinted above.

Multiple copies and systematic reproduction

Subsection (g) provides that the rights granted by this section extend only to the "isolated and unrelated reproduction of a single copy or phonorecord of the same material on separate occasions." However, this section does not authorize the related or concerted reproduction of multiple copies or phonorecords of the same material, whether made on one occasion or over a period of time, and whether intended for aggregate use by one individual or for separate use by the individual members of a group.

With respect to material described in subsection (d)—articles or other contributions to periodicals or collections, and small parts of other copyrighted works—subsection (g)(2) provides that the exemptions of section 108 do not apply if the library or archives engages in "systematic reproduction or distribution of single or multiple copies or phonorecords." This provision in S.22 provoked a storm of controversy, centering around the extent to which the restrictions on "systematic" activities would prevent the continuation and development of interlibrary networks and other arrangements involving the exchange of photocopies. After thorough consideration, the Committee amended section 108 (g)(2) to add the following proviso:

Provided, that nothing in this clause prevents a library or archives from participating in interlibrary arrangements that do not have, as their purpose or effect, that the library or archives receiving such copies or phonorecords for distribution does so in such aggregate quantities as to substitute for a subscription to or purchase of such work.

In addition, the Committee added a new subsection (i) to section 108, requiring the Register of Copyrights, five years from the effective date of the new Act and at five-year intervals thereafter, to report to Congress upon "the extent to which this section has achieved the intended statutory balancing of the rights of creators, and the needs of users," and to make appropriate legislative or other recommendations. As noted in connection with section 107, the Committee also amended section 504(c) in a way that would insulate librarians from unwarranted liability for copyright infringement; this amendment is discussed below.

The key phrases in the Committee's amendment of section 108(g)(2) are "aggregate quantities" and "substitute for a subscription to or purchase of" a work. To be implemented effectively in practice, these provisions will require the development and implementation of more-or-less specific guidelines establishing criteria to govern various situations.

The National Commission on New Technological Uses of Copyrighted Works (CONTU) offered to provide good offices in helping to develop these guidelines. This offer was accepted and, although the final text of guidelines has not yet been achieved, the Committee has reason to hope that, within the next month, some agreement can be reached on an initial set of guidelines covering practices under section 108(g)(2).

f. House Report: Discussion of Works Excluded

The House Report's discussion of section 108(h) is longer than the corresponding paragraph in the Senate Report, and reflects certain amendments in the subsection.

Works excluded
Subsection (h) provides that the rights of reproduction and distribution under this section do not apply to a musical work, a pictorial, graphic or sculptural work, or a motion picture or other audiovisual work other than "an audiovisual work dealing with news." The latter term is intended as the equivalent in meaning of the phrase "audiovisual news program" in section 108(f)(3). The exclusions under subsection (h) do not apply to archival reproduction under subsection (b), to replacement of damaged or lost copies or phonorecords under subsection (c), or to "pictorial or graphic works published as illustrations, diagrams, or similar adjuncts to works of which copies are reproduced or distributed in accordance with subsections (d) and (e)."

Although subsection (h) generally removes musical, graphic, and audiovisual works from the specific exemptions of section 108, it is important to recognize that the doctrine of fair use under section 107 remains fully applicable to the photocopying or other reproduction of such works. In the case of music, for example, it would be fair use for a scholar doing musicological research to have a library supply a copy of a portion of a score or to reproduce portions of a phonorecord of a work. Nothing in section 108 impairs the applicability of the fair use doctrine to a wide variety of situations involving photocopying or other reproduction by a library of copyrighted material in its collections, where the user requests the reproduction for legitimate scholarly or research purposes.

III. EXCERPTS FROM CONFERENCE REPORT

The following excerpt is reprinted from the Report of the Conference Committee on the new copyright law (H.R. Rep. No. 94-1733, pages 70-74).

a. Conference Report: Introductory Discussion of Section 108

Reproduction by Libraries and Archives

Senate bill
Section 108 of the Senate bill dealt with a variety of situations involving photocopying and other forms of reproduction by libraries and archives. It specified the conditions under which single copies of copyrighted material can be noncommercially reproduced and distributed, but made clear that the privileges of a library or archives under the section do not apply where the reproduction or distribution

is of multiple copies or is "systematic." Under subsection (f), the section was not to be construed as limiting the reproduction and distribution, by a library or archives meeting the basic criteria of the section, of a limited number of copies and excerpts of an audiovisual news program.

House bill

The House bill amended section 108 to make clear that, in cases involving interlibrary arrangements for the exchange of photocopies, the activity would not be considered "systematic" as long as the library or archives receiving the reproductions for distribution does not do so in such aggregate quantities as to substitute for a subscription to or purchase of the work. A new subsection (i) directed the Register of Copyrights, by the end of 1982 and at five-year intervals thereafter, to report on the practical success of the section in balancing the various interests, and to make recommendations for any needed changes. With respect to audiovisual news programs, the House bill limited the scope of the distribution privilege confirmed by section 108 (f)(3) to cases where the distribution takes the form of a loan.

b. Conference Report: Conference Committee Discussion of CONTU Guidelines on Photocopying and Interlibrary arrangements

Conference substitute

The conference substitute adopts the provisions of section 108 as amended by the House bill. In doing so, the conferees have noted two letters dated September 22, 1976, sent respectively to John L. McClellan, Chairman of the Senate Judiciary Subcommittee on Patents, Trademarks, and Copyrights, and to Robert W. Kastenmeier, Chairman of the House Judiciary Subcommittee on Courts, Civil Liberties, and the Administration of Justice. The letters, from the Chairman of the National Commission on New Technological Uses of Copyrighted Works (CONTU), Stanley H. Fuld, transmitted a document consisting of "guidelines interpreting the provision in subsection 108 (g)(2) of S.22, as approved by the House Committee on the Judiciary." Chairman Fuld's letters explain that, following lengthy consultations with the parties concerned, the Commission adopted these guidelines as fair and workable and with the hope that the conferees on S.22 may find that they merit inclusion in the conference report. The letters add that, although time did not permit securing signatures of the representatives of the principal library organizations or of the organizations representing publishers and authors on these guidelines, the Commission had received oral assurances from these representatives that the guidelines are acceptable to their organizations.

The conference committee understands that the guidelines are not intended as, and cannot be considered, explicit rules or directions governing any and all cases, now or in the future. It is recognized that their purpose is to provide guidance in the most commonly-encountered interlibrary photocopying situations, that they are not intended to be limiting or determinative in themselves or with respect to other situations, and that they deal with an evolving situation that will undoubtedly require their continuous reevaluation and adjustment. With these qualifications, the conference committee agrees that the guidelines are a reasonable interpretation of the proviso of section 108 (g)(2) in the most common situations to which they apply today.

c. Conference Report: Reprint of CONTU Guidelines on Photocopying and Interlibrary Arrangements

The text of the guidelines follows:

Photocopying—Interlibrary Arrangements

Introduction
Subsection 108 (g) (2) of the bill deals, among other things, with limits on interlibrary arrangements for photocopying. It prohibits systematic photocopying of copyrighted materials but permits interlibrary arrangements "that do not have, as their purposes or effect, that the library or archives receiving such copies or phonorecords for distribution does so in such aggregate quantities as to substitute for a subscription to or purchase of such work."

The National Commission on New Technological Uses of Copyrighted Works offered its good offices to the House and Senate subcommittees in bringing the interested parties together to see if agreement could be reached on what a realistic definition would be of "such aggregate quantities." The Commission consulted with the parties and suggested the interpretation which follows, on which there has been substantial agreement by the principal library, publisher, and author organizations. The Commission considers the guidelines which follow to be a workable and fair interpretation of the intent of the proviso portion of subsection 108 (g)(2).

These guidelines are intended to provide guidance in the application of section 108 to the most frequently encountered interlibrary case: a library's obtaining from another library, in lieu of interlibrary loan, copies of articles from relatively recent issues of periodicals—those published within five years prior to the date of the request. The guidelines do not specify what aggregate quantity of copies of an article or articles published in a periodical, the issue date of which is more than five years prior to the date when the request for the copy thereof is made, constitutes a substitute for a subscription to such periodical. The meaning of the proviso to subsection 108 (g)(2) in such case is left to future interpretation.

The point has been made that the present practice on interlibrary loans and use of photocopies in lieu of loans may be supplemented or even largely replaced by a system in which one or more agencies or institutions, public or private, exist for the specific purpose of providing a central source for photocopies. Of course, these guidelines would not apply to such a situation.

Guidelines for the Proviso of Subsection 108(G)(2)

1. As used in the proviso of subsection 108 (g)(2), the words ". . .such aggregate quantities as to substitute for a subscription to or purchase of such work" shall mean:

(a) with respect to any given periodical (as opposed to any given issue of a periodical), filled requests of a library or archives (a "requesting entity") within any calendar year for a total of six or more copies of an article or articles published in such periodical within five years prior to the date of the request. These guidelines specifically shall not apply, directly or indirectly, to any request of a requesting entity for a copy or copies of an article or articles published in any issue of a periodical, the publication date of which is more than five years prior to the date when the request is made. The guidelines do not define the meaning, with respect to such a request, of ". . .such aggregate quantities as to substitute for a subscription to (such periodical)".

(b) With respect to any other material described in subsection 108 (d), (including fiction and poetry), filled requests of a requesting entity within any calendar year for a total of six or more copies or phonorecords of or from any given work (including a collective work) during the entire period when such material shall be protected by copyright.

2. In the event that a requesting entity

(a) shall have in force or shall have entered an order for a subscription to a periodical, or

(b) has within its collection, or shall have entered an order for, a copy or phonorecord of any other copyrighted work, material from either category of which it desires to obtain by copy from another library or archives (the "supplying entity"), because the material to be copied is not reasonably available for use by the requesting entity itself, then the fulfillment of such request shall be treated as though the requesting entity made such copy from its own collection. A library or archives may request a copy or phonorecord from a supplying entity only under those circumstances where the requesting entity would have been able, under the other provisions of section 108, to supply such copy from materials in its own collection.

3. No request for a copy or phonorecord of any material to which these guidelines apply may be fulfilled by the supplying entity unless such request is accompanied by a representation by the requesting entity that the request was made in conformity with these guidelines.

4. The requesting entity shall maintain records of all requests made by it for copies or phonorecords of any materials to which these guidelines apply and shall maintain records of the fulfillment of such requests, which records shall be retained until the end of the third complete calendar year after the end of the calendar year in which the respective request shall have been made.

5. As part of the review provided for in subsection 108 (i), these guidelines shall be reviewed not later than five years from the effective date of this bill.

d. Conference Report: Discussion of "Audiovisual News Program"

The conference committee is aware that an issue has arisen as to the meaning of the phrase "audiovisual news program" in section 108 (f) (3). The conferees believe that, under the provision as adopted in the conference substitute, a library or archives qualifying under section 108 (a) would be free, without regard to the archival activities of the Library of Congress or any other organization, to reproduce, on videotape or any other medium of fixation or reproduction, local, regional, or network newscasts, interviews concerning current news events, and on-the-spot coverage of news events, and to distribute a limited number of reproductions of such a program on a loan basis.

e. Conference Report: Discussion of Libraries and Archives in Profit-making Institutions

Another point of interpretation involves the meaning of "indirect commercial advantage," as used in section 108 (a)(1), in the case of libraries or archival collections within industrial, profit-making, or proprietary institutions. As long as the library or archives meets the criteria in section 108 (a) and the other requirements of the section, including the prohibitions against multiple and systematic copying in subsection (g), the conferees consider that the isolated, spontaneous making of single photocopies by a library or archives in a for-profit organization without any commercial motivation, or participation by such a library or archives in interlibrary arrangements, would come within the scope of section 108.

Appendix E

COPYRIGHT REMEDY CLARIFICATION ACT

PUBLIC LAW 101-553 (H.R. 3045); November 15, 1990

An Act to amend chapters 5 and 9 of title 17, United States Code, to clarify that States, instrumentalities of States, and officers and employees of States acting in their official capacity, are subject to suit in Federal court by any person for infringement of copyright and infringement of exclusive rights in mask works, and that all the remedies can be obtained in such suit that can be obtained in a suit against a private person or against other public entities.

Be it enacted by the Senate and House of Representatives of the United States of America in Congress assembled.

SECTION 1. SHORT TITLE.

This Act may be cited as the "Copyright Remedy Clarification Act."

SEC. 2. LIABILITY OF STATES, INSTRUMENTALITIES OF STATES, AND STATE OFFICIALS FOR INFRINGEMENT OF COPYRIGHT AND EXCLUSIVE RIGHTS IN MASK WORKS.

(a) COPYRIGHT INFRINGEMENT.—(1) Section 501(a) of title 17, United States Code, is amended by adding at the end the following: "As used in this subsection, the term 'anyone' includes any State, any instrumentality of a State, and any officer or employee of a State or instrumentality of a State acting in his or her official capacity. Any State, and any such instrumentality, officer, or employee, shall be subject to the provisions of this title in the same manner and to the same extent as any nongovernmental entity." (2) Chapter 5 of title 17, United States Code, is amended by adding at the end the following new section:

§511. Liability of States, instrumentalities of States, and State officials for infringement of copyright

(a) IN GENERAL.—Any State, any instrumentality of a State, and any officer or employee of a State or instrumentality of a State acting in his or her official capacity, shall not be immune, under the Eleventh Amendment of the Constitution of the United States or under any other doctrine of sovereign immunity, from suit in Federal court by any person, including any governmental or nongovernmental entity, for a violation of any of the exclusive rights of a copyright owner provided by sections 106 through 119, for importing copies of phonorecords in violation of section 602,or for any other violation under this title.

(b) REMEDIES.—In a suit described in subsection (a) for a violation described in that subsection, remedies (including remedies both at law and in equity) are available for the violation to the same extent as such remedies are available for such a violation in a suit against any public or private entity other than a State, instrumentality of a State, or officer or employee of a State acting in his or her official capacity. Such remedies include impounding and disposition of infringing articles under section 503, actual damages and profits and statutory damages under section 504, costs and attorney's fees under section 505, and the remedies provided in section 510.

(3) The table of sections at the beginning of chapter 5 of title 17, United States Code, is amended by adding at the end the following new item:

"Sec 511 Liability of States, instrumentalities of States, and State officials for infringement of copyright."

(b) INFRINGEMENT OF EXCLUSIVE RIGHTS IN MASK WORKS.—
(1) Section 910(a) of title 17, United States Code, is amended by adding at the end the following: "as used in this subsection, the term 'any person' includes any State, any instrumentality of a State, and any officer or employee of a State or instrumentality of a State acting in his or her official capacity. Any State, and any such instrumentality, officer, or employee, shall be subject to the provisions of this chapter in the same manner and to the same extent as any non-governmental entity."

(2) Section 911 of title 17, United States Code, is amended by adding at the end the following new subsection:

(g)(1) Any State, any instrumentality of a State, and any officer or employee of a State or instrumentality of a State acting in his or her official capacity, shall not be immune, under the Eleventh Amendment of the Constitution of the United States or under any other doctrine of sovereign immunity, from suit in Federal court by any person, including any governmental or nongovernmental entity, for a violation of any of the exclusive rights of the owner of a mask work under this chapter, or for any other violation under this chapter.

(2) In a suit described in paragraph (1) for a violation described in that paragraph, remedies (including remedies both at law and in equity) are available for the violation to the same extent as such remedies are available for such a violation in a suit against any public or private entity other than a State, instrumentality of a State, or officer or employee of a State acting in his or her official capacity. Such remedies include actual damages and profits under subsection (b), statutory damages under subsection (c), impounding and disposition of infringing articles under subsection (e), and costs and attorney's fees under subsection (f).

SEC. 3. EFFECTIVE DATE.

The amendments made by this Act shall take effect with respect to violations that occur on or after the date of the enactment of this Act.

Approved November 15, 1990.

Appendix F

CONTU GUIDELINES:

Full Text

National Commission on New Technological Uses of Copyrighted Works [CONTU] offered its good offices to the House and Senate subcommittee in bringing the interested parties together to see if agreement could be reached on what a realistic definition would be of "such aggregate quantities." The Commission consulted with the parties and suggested the interpretation which follows, on which there has been substantial agreement by the principal library, publisher, and author organizations. The Commission considers the guidelines which follow to be a workable and fair interpretation of the intent of the proviso portion of subsection 108(g)(2).

1. As used in the proviso of subsection 108(g)(2), the words ". . . such aggregate quantities as to substitute for a subscription to or purchase of such work "shall mean:

(a) with respect to any given periodical (as opposed to any given issue of a periodical), filled requests of a library or archive (a "requesting entity") within any calendar year for a total of six or more copies of an article or articles published in such periodical within five years prior to the date of the request. These guidelines specifically shall not apply, directly or indirectly, to any request of a requesting entity for a copy or copies of an article or articles published in any issue of a periodical, the publication date of which is more than five years prior to the date when the request is made. These guidelines do not define the meaning with respect to such a request, of " . . . such aggregate quantities as to substitute for a subscription to."

(b) With respect to any other material described in subsection 108(d), (including fiction and poetry), filled requests of a requesting entity within

134

any calendar year for a total of six or more copies or phonorecords of or from any given work (including a collective work) during the entire period when such material shall be protected by copyright.

2. In the event that a requesting entity—

(a) shall have in force or shall have entered an order for a subscription to a periodical, or

(b) has within its collection, or shall have entered an order for, a copy or phonorecord of any other copyrighted work, material from either category of which it desires to obtain by copy from another library or archive(the "supplying entity"), because the material to be copied is not reasonably available for use by the requesting entity itself, then the fulfillment of such request shall be treated as though the requesting entity made such copy from its own collection. A library or archives may request a copy or phonorecord from a supplying entity only under those circumstances where the requesting entity would have been able, under the other provisions of section 108, to supply such copy from materials from its own collection.

3. No request for a copy or phonorecord of any material to which these guidelines apply may be fulfilled by the supplying entity unless such request is accompanied by a representation by the requesting entity that the request was made in conformity with these guidelines.

4. The requesting entity shall maintain records of all requests made by it for copies or phonorecords of any materials to which these guidelines apply and shall maintain records of the fulfillment of such requests, which records shall be retained until the end of the third complete calendar year in which the respective request shall have been made.

5. As part of the review provided for in subsection 108(i), these guidelines shall be reviewed not later than five years from the effective date of this bill.

Appendix G

§ 504 INNOCENT INFRINGEMENT BY LIBRARY OR NONPROFIT EDUCATIONAL INSTITUTION

(a) IN GENERAL.—Except as otherwise provided by this title, an infringer of copyright is liable for either—

(1) The copyright owner's actual damages and any additional profits of the infringer, as provided by subsection (b); or

(2) statutory damages, as provided by subsection (c).

(b) Actual Damages and Profits.—The Copyright owner is entitled to recover the actual damages suffered by him or her as a result of the infringement, and any profits of the infringer that are attributable to the infringement and are not taken into account in computing the actual damages. In establishing the infringer's profits, the copyright owner is required to present proof only of the infringer's gross revenue, and the infringer is required to prove his or her deductible expenses and the elements of profit attributable to factors other than the copyrighted work.

(c) Statutory Damages.—

(1) Except as provided by clause (2) of this subsection, the Copyright owner may elect, at any time before final judgment is rendered, to recover, instead of actual damages and profits, an award of statutory damages for all infringements involved in the action, with respect to any one work, for which any one infringer is liable individually, or for which any two or more infringers are liable jointly and severally, in a sum of not less than $250 or more than $10,000 as the court considers just. For the purposes of this subsection, all the parts of a compilation or derivative work constitute one work.

(2) In a case where the copyright owner sustains the burden of proving,

and the court finds, that infringement was committed willfully, the court in its discretion may increase the award of statutory damages to a sum of not more than $50,000. In a case where the infringer sustains the burden of proving, and the court finds, that such infringer was not aware and had no reason to believe that his or her acts constituted an infringement of copyright, the court in its discretion may reduce the award of statutory damages to a sum of not less than $100. The court shall remit statutory damages in any case where an infringer believed and had reasonable ground that his or her use of the copyrighted work was a fair use under section 107, if the infringer was: (i) an employee or agent of a nonprofit educational institution, library, or archives acting within the scope of his or her employment who, or such institution, library, or archives itself, which infringed by reproducing the work in copies or phonorecords; or (ii) a public broadcasting entity which or a person who, as a regular part of the nonprofit activities of a public broadcasting entity (as defined in subsection (g) of section 118) infringed by performing a published nondramatic literary work or by reproducing a transmission program embodying a performance of such a work.

Appendix H

COMPUTER SOFTWARE RENTAL AMENDMENTS
ACT OF 1989

S.198, 101st Congress, 2d Session

IN THE HOUSE OF REPRESENTATIVES

MAY 3, 1990

REFERRED TO THE COMMITTEE ON THE JUDICIARY

AN ACT

To amend title 17, United States Code, the Copyright Act to protect certain computer programs.

Be it enacted by the Senate and House of Representatives of the United States of America in Congress assembled, That this act may be cited as the "Computer Software Rental Amendments Act of 1989".

SEC. 2. Section 109(b) of title 17, United States Code, is amended by—

(1) amending paragraph (1) to read as follows:

"(b)(1)(A) Notwithstanding the provisions of subsection (a), unless authorized by the owners of copyright in the sound recording or the owner of copyright in a computer program (including any tape, disk, or other medium embodying such program), and in the case of a sound recording in the musical words embodied therein, neither the owner of a particular phonorecord nor any person in possession of a particular copy of a computer program (including any tape, disk, or other medium embodying such program), may, for the purposes of direct or indirect commercial advantage, dispose of, or authorize the disposal of, the possession of that phonorecord or computer program (including any tape, disk, or other medium embodying such program) by rental, lease, or lending, or by any other act or practice in the nature of rental, lease, or lending. Nothing in the preceding sentence shall apply to the rental, lease, or lending of a phonorecord for nonprofit purposes by a nonprofit library or nonprofit educational institution. The transfer of possession of a lawfully made copy of a computer program by a nonprofit educational institution to another nonprofit educational institution or to faculty, staff and students does not constitute rental, lease or lending for direct or indirect commercial purposes under this Act.

"(B) The term 'computer program', for purposes of this subsection, does not include any computer program embodied in electronic circuitry which is contained in, or used in conjunction with, a limited purpose computer designed primarily for playing home video games.";

(2) redesignating paragraphs (2) and (3), as paragraphs (3) and (4), respectively;

(3) inserting between paragraph (1) and paragraph (3), as redesignated herein, the following:

"(2)(A) Nothing in this subsection shall apply to the lending of a computer program by a nonprofit library, providing that each copy of a copyrighted computer program which is lent by such library shall have affixed to the packaging containing the program the following notice:

WARNING: THIS COMPUTER PROGRAM IS PROTECTED UNDER THE COPYRIGHT LAW. MAKING A COPY OF THIS PROGRAM WITHOUT PERMISSION OF THE COPYRIGHT OWNER IS PROHIBITED. ANYONE COPYING THIS PROGRAM WITHOUT PERMISSION OF THE COPYRIGHT OWNER MAY BE SUBJECT TO PAYMENT OF UP TO $100,000 DAMAGES AND, IN SOME CASES, IMPRISONMENT FOR UP TO ONE YEAR.

"(B) Three years after the effective date of this paragraph, and at such times subsequently as he or she may deem appropriate, the Register of Copyrights, after consultation with representatives of copyright owners and librarians, shall submit to the Congress a report stating whether the provisions of this paragraph have achieved the intended purpose of maintaining the integrity of the copyright system while providing nonprofit libraries the capability to fulfill their function. Such report shall advise the Congress as to any information or recommendations the Register of Copyrights shall deem necessary to effectuate the purposes of this Act."; and (4) amending paragraph (4) to read as follows:

"(4) Any person who distributes a phonorecord or a copy of a computer program (including any tape, disk, or other medium embodying such program) in violation of clause (1) is an infringer of copyright under section 501 of this title and is subject to the remedies set forth in sections 502, 503, 504, 505, and 509. Such violation shall not be a criminal offense under section 506 or cause such person to be subject to the criminal penalties set forth in section 2319 of title 18."

Passed the Senate May 1 (legislative day, April 18), 1990.

Attest: WALTER J. STEWART, Secretary.

Index